Just The facts101 Textbook Key Facts

Bundle: Microeconomics For Today 6E

by Cram101
Texbook NOT Included

Table of Contents

Just The Facts101

Exam Prep for

Bundle: Microeconomics For Today
6E

Just The Facts101 Exam Prep is your link from
the textbook and lecture to your exams.

**Just The Facts101 Exam Preps are unauthorized and comprehensive reviews
of your textbooks.**

Just The Facts101 Exam Prep

Copyright © 2019 by CTI Publications. All rights reserved.

eAIN 458743

Introduction to economics

Prices and quantities have been described as the most directly observable attributes of goods produced and exchanged in a market economy. The theory of supply and demand is an organizing principle for explaining how prices coordinate the amounts produced and consumed.

:: Crisis ::

A _____ is any event that is going to lead to an unstable and dangerous situation affecting an individual, group, community, or whole society. Crises are deemed to be negative changes in the security, economic, political, societal, or environmental affairs, especially when they occur abruptly, with little or no warning. More loosely, it is a term meaning "a testing time" or an "emergency event".

Exam Probability: **Medium**

1. *Answer choices:*

(see index for correct answer)

- a. Crisis plan
- b. International crisis
- c. Situational crisis communication theory
- d. Crisis management

Guidance: level 1

:: National accounts ::

A _____ consists of one people who live in the same dwelling and share meals. It may also consist of a single family or another group of people. A dwelling is considered to contain multiple _____ s if meals or living spaces are not shared. The _____ is the basic unit of analysis in many social, microeconomic and government models, and is important to economics and inheritance.

Exam Probability: **High**

2. *Answer choices:*

(see index for correct answer)

- a. Household
- b. Gross national income
- c. Real gross domestic product
- d. Operating surplus

:: Production economics ::

In economics long run is a theoretical concept where all markets are in equilibrium, and all prices and quantities have fully adjusted and are in equilibrium. The long run contrasts with the _____ where there are some constraints and markets are not fully in equilibrium.

Exam Probability: **Low**

3. *Answer choices:*

(see index for correct answer)

- a. Constant elasticity of transformation
- b. Short run
- c. Programming productivity
- d. Economic batch quantity

:: Labor economics ::

The workforce or labour force is the labour pool in employment. It is generally used to describe those working for a single company or industry, but can also apply to a geographic region like a city, state, or country. Within a company, its value can be labelled as its "Workforce in Place". The workforce of a country includes both the employed and the unemployed. The labour force participation rate, LFPR , is the ratio between the labour force and the overall size of their cohort . The term generally excludes the employers or management, and can imply those involved in manual labour. It may also mean all those who are available for work.

Exam Probability: **Medium**

4. *Answer choices:*

(see index for correct answer)

- a. Labor force
- b. labor force participation rate
- c. Primary labor market
- d. Full Employment in a Free Society

Guidance: level 1

:: Property law ::

_____ is a legal designation for the ownership of property by non-governmental legal entities. _____ is distinguishable from public property, which is owned by a state entity; and from collective property, which is owned by a group of non-governmental entities. _____ can be either personal property or capital goods. _____ is a legal concept defined and enforced by a country's political system.

Exam Probability: **Low**

5. *Answer choices:*

(see index for correct answer)

- a. Private property
- b. Constructive eviction
- c. Dominium
- d. Condition subsequent

Guidance: level 1

:: Export ::

An _____ in international trade is a good or service produced in one country that is bought by someone in another country. The seller of such goods and services is an _____ er; the foreign buyer is an importer.

Exam Probability: **Low**

6. *Answer choices:*

(see index for correct answer)

- a. Export variants of Soviet military equipment
- b. Export
- c. Export hay

Guidance: level 1

:: Demand ::

In economics, supply is the amount of a resource that firms, producers, labourers, providers of financial assets, or other economic agents are willing and able to provide to the marketplace or directly to another agent in the marketplace. Supply can be in currency, time, raw materials, or any other scarce or valuable object that can be provided to another agent. This is often fairly abstract. For example in the case of time, supply is not transferred to one agent from another, but one agent may offer some other resource in exchange for the first spending time doing something. Supply is often plotted graphically with the quantity provided plotted horizontally and the price plotted vertically.

Exam Probability: **Medium**

7. *Answer choices:*

(see index for correct answer)

- a. Supply creates its own demand
- b. Wealth elasticity of demand

- c. Marginal demand
- d. price function

Guidance: level 1

:: Monetary policy ::

In monetary economics, a _____ is one of various closely related ratios of commercial bank money to central bank money under a fractional-reserve banking system. In one version it measures the maximum amount of commercial bank money that can be created, given a certain amount of central bank money and ignoring leakages into currency held by the non-bank public. That is, in a fractional-reserve banking system, the total amount of loans that commercial banks are allowed to extend when there are no leakages is equal to a multiple of the amount of reserves. This multiple is the reciprocal of the reserve ratio, and it is an economic multiplier. The actual ratio of money to central bank money, also called the _____ , is lower because some funds are held by the non-bank public as currency and most banks hold excess reserves

Exam Probability: **Medium**

8. *Answer choices:*

(see index for correct answer)

- a. Lombard credit
- b. market monetarist
- c. Zero lower bound problem
- d. discretionary policy

:: Microeconomics ::

In economics, _____ is the total economic cost of production and is made up of variable cost, which varies according to the quantity of a good produced and includes inputs such as labour and raw materials, plus fixed cost, which is independent of the quantity of a good produced and includes inputs that cannot be varied in the short term: fixed costs such as buildings and machinery, including sunk costs if any. Since cost is measured per unit of time, it is a flow variable.

Exam Probability: **Low**

9. *Answer choices:*

(see index for correct answer)

- a. Total cost
- b. Marginal profit
- c. Schedule delay
- d. Oligopsony

:: Goods ::

_____ s or producer goods or semi-finished products are goods, such as partly finished goods, used as inputs in the production of other goods including final goods. A firm may make and then use _____ s, or make and then sell, or buy then use them. In the production process, _____ s either become part of the final product, or are changed beyond recognition in the process. This means _____ s are resold among industries.

Exam Probability: **Medium**

10. *Answer choices:*

(see index for correct answer)

- a. Intermediate good
- b. Veblen effect
- c. Composite good
- d. Search good

Guidance: level 1

:: International economics ::

In finance, an _____ is the rate at which one currency will be exchanged for another. It is also regarded as the value of one country's currency in relation to another currency. For example, an interbank _____ of 114 Japanese yen to the United States dollar means that ¥114 will be exchanged for each US$1 or that US$1 will be exchanged for each ¥114. In this case it is said that the price of a dollar in relation to yen is ¥114, or equivalently that the price of a yen in relation to dollars is $1/114.

11. *Answer choices:*

(see index for correct answer)

- a. Small open economy
- b. Counterpart fund
- c. Rybczynski theorem
- d. Remittance

Guidance: level 1

:: Decision theory ::

_____ involves decision making. It can include judging the merits of multiple options and selecting one or more of them. One can make a _____ between imagined options or between real options followed by the corresponding action. For example, a traveler might choose a route for a journey based on the preference of arriving at a given destination as soon as possible. The preferred route can then follow from information such as the length of each of the possible routes, traffic conditions, etc. The arrival at a _____ can include more complex motivators such as cognition, instinct, and feeling.

12. *Answer choices:*

(see index for correct answer)

- a. Rulemaking
- b. Choice
- c. Consensus decision-making
- d. Decision analysis cycle

Guidance: level 1

:: Operations research ::

_____ or stock is the goods and materials that a business holds for the ultimate goal of resale .

Exam Probability: **High**

13. *Answer choices:*

(see index for correct answer)

- a. Interfaces
- b. Government Operational Research Service
- c. Monge array
- d. Dynamic simulation

Guidance: level 1

:: Marginal concepts ::

In economics, utility is the satisfaction or benefit derived by consuming a product; thus the _____ of a good or service is the change in the utility from an increase in the consumption of that good or service.

Exam Probability: **High**

14. *Answer choices:*

(see index for correct answer)

- a. Marginal use
- b. technical rate of substitution
- c. Marginal concepts
- d. Marginal utility

Guidance: level 1

:: Goods ::

In economics, a _____ is a good that is both non-excludable and non-rivalrous in that individuals cannot be excluded from use or could be enjoyed without paying for it, and where use by one individual does not reduce availability to others or the goods can be effectively consumed simultaneously by more than one person. This is in contrast to a common good which is non-excludable but is rivalrous to a certain degree.

Exam Probability: **Low**

15. *Answer choices:*

(see index for correct answer)

- a. Public good
- b. Superior good
- c. Positional good
- d. Cargo

Guidance: level 1

:: Dividends ::

A _____ is a payment made by a corporation to its shareholders, usually as a distribution of profits. When a corporation earns a profit or surplus, the corporation is able to re-invest the profit in the business and pay a proportion of the profit as a _____ to shareholders. Distribution to shareholders may be in cash or, if the corporation has a _____ reinvestment plan, the amount can be paid by the issue of further shares or share repurchase. When _____ s are paid, shareholders typically must pay income taxes, and the corporation does not receive a corporate income tax deduction for the _____ payments.

Exam Probability: **Low**

16. *Answer choices:*

(see index for correct answer)

- a. Division 7A dividend
- b. Dividend imputation

- c. Dividend
- d. Dividend distribution tax

Guidance: level 1

:: Stock market ::

_____ is freedom from, or resilience against, potential harm caused by others. Beneficiaries of _____ may be of persons and social groups, objects and institutions, ecosystems or any other entity or phenomenon vulnerable to unwanted change by its environment.

Exam Probability: **High**

17. *Answer choices:*

(see index for correct answer)

- a. GXG Markets
- b. Direct participation program
- c. Matchbook FX
- d. Security

Guidance: level 1

:: Money ::

In economics, _____ is money in the physical form of currency, such as banknotes and coins. In bookkeeping and finance, _____ is current assets comprising currency or currency equivalents that can be accessed immediately or near-immediately . _____ is seen either as a reserve for payments, in case of a structural or incidental negative _____ flow or as a way to avoid a downturn on financial markets.

Exam Probability: **Low**

18. *Answer choices:*

(see index for correct answer)

- a. Ideal money
- b. Play money
- c. Money burning
- d. Cash

Guidance: level 1

:: Production economics ::

In economics and in particular neoclassical economics, the _____ or marginal physical productivity of an input is the change in output resulting from employing one more unit of a particular input , assuming that the quantities of other inputs are kept constant.

Exam Probability: **High**

19. *Answer choices:*

(see index for correct answer)

- a. Theory of non-constraint
- b. Split-off point
- c. Synergy
- d. Specialization

Guidance: level 1

:: Political economy ::

In economics, _____ , or recession-inflation, is a situation in which the inflation rate is high, the economic growth rate slows, and unemployment remains steadily high. It presents a dilemma for economic policy, since actions intended to lower inflation may exacerbate unemployment, and vice versa.

Exam Probability: **Medium**

20. *Answer choices:*

(see index for correct answer)

- a. New political economy
- b. Stagflation
- c. Royal Arsenal Co-operative Society
- d. Organic composition of capital

:: Rational choice theory ::

In economics, " _____ " are model-consistent expectations, in that agents inside the model are assumed to "know the model" and on average take the model's predictions as valid. _____ ensure internal consistency in models involving uncertainty. To obtain consistency within a model, the predictions of future values of economically relevant variables from the model are assumed to be the same as that of the decision-makers in the model, given their information set, the nature of the random processes involved, and model structure. The _____ assumption is used especially in many contemporary macroeconomic models.

Exam Probability: **High**

21. *Answer choices:*

(see index for correct answer)

- a. Michael Taylor
- b. The Logic of Collective Action
- c. Rational expectations
- d. Making Sense of Marx

:: Public administration ::

_____ is the stock of habits, knowledge, social and personality attributes embodied in the ability to perform labor so as to produce economic value.

Exam Probability: **High**

22. *Answer choices:*

(see index for correct answer)

- a. De-Mail
- b. Human capital
- c. Lean Government
- d. Professional administration

Guidance: level 1

:: Microeconomics ::

In microeconomics, the _____ states that, "conditional on all else being equal, as the price of a good increases , quantity demanded decreases ; conversely, as the price of a good decreases , quantity demanded ". In other words, the _____ describes an inverse relationship between price and quantity demanded of a good. Alternatively, other things being constant, quantity demanded of a commodity is inversely related to the price of the commodity. For example, a consumer may demand 2 kilograms of apples at $70 per kg; he may, however, demand 1 kg if the price rises to $80 per kg. This has been the general human behaviour on relationship between the price of the commodity and the quantity demanded. The factors held constant refer to other determinants of demand, such as the prices of other goods and the consumer`s income. There are, however, some possible exceptions to the _____ , such as Giffen goods and Veblen goods.

Exam Probability: **High**

23. *Answer choices:*

(see index for correct answer)

- a. Dollar voting
- b. Microeconomic reform
- c. Oligopsony
- d. Law of demand

Guidance: level 1

:: Game theory ::

In game theory, the _____ , named after the mathematician John Forbes Nash Jr., is a proposed solution of a non-cooperative game involving two or more players in which each player is assumed to know the equilibrium strategies of the other players, and no player has anything to gain by changing only their own strategy.

Exam Probability: **Low**

24. *Answer choices:*

(see index for correct answer)

- a. Competitive altruism
- b. Truel
- c. Nash equilibrium
- d. Punctuality

Guidance: level 1

:: Great Depression ::

The _____ was a severe worldwide economic depression that took place mostly during the 1930s, beginning in the United States. The timing of the _____ varied across nations; in most countries it started in 1929 and lasted until the late-1930s. It was the longest, deepest, and most widespread depression of the 20th century. In the 21st century, the _____ is commonly used as an example of how intensely the world`s economy can decline.

Exam Probability: **Low**

25. *Answer choices:*

(see index for correct answer)

- a. Boondoggle
- b. Great Contraction
- c. Great Depression
- d. Yanks for Stalin

Guidance: level 1

:: Socioeconomics ::

Economic interventionism is an economic policy perspective favoring _____ in the market process to correct the market failures and promote the general welfare of the people. An economic intervention is an action taken by a government or international institution in a market economy in an effort to impact the economy beyond the basic regulation of fraud and enforcement of contracts and provision of public goods. Economic intervention can be aimed at a variety of political or economic objectives, such as promoting economic growth, increasing employment, raising wages, raising or reducing prices, promoting income equality, managing the money supply and interest rates, increasing profits, or addressing market failures.

Exam Probability: **High**

26. *Answer choices:*

(see index for correct answer)

- a. Community health

- b. Government intervention
- c. Class analysis
- d. Anticipatory socialization

Guidance: level 1

:: Rent regulation ::

Rent regulation is a system of laws, administered by a court or a public authority, which aim to ensure the affordability of housing and tenancies on the rental market for dwellings. Generally, a system of rent regulation involves.

Exam Probability: **High**

27. *Answer choices:*

(see index for correct answer)

- a. Block v. Hirsh
- b. Citizens Against Rent Control v. City of Berkeley
- c. Rent control in Ontario
- d. Rent regulation in Canada

Guidance: level 1

:: Communism ::

In political and social sciences, _____ is the philosophical, social, political, and economic ideology and movement whose ultimate goal is the establishment of the communist society, which is a socioeconomic order structured upon the common ownership of the means of production and the absence of social classes, money, and the state.

Exam Probability: **High**

28. *Answer choices:*

(see index for correct answer)

- a. Jewish Bolshevism
- b. Kolejka
- c. Communism
- d. Ideology of the Communist Party of China

Guidance: level 1

:: Monetary policy ::

_____ is the process by which the monetary authority of a country, typically the central bank or currency board, controls either the cost of very short-term borrowing or the money supply, often targeting inflation rate or interest rate to ensure price stability and general trust in the currency.

Exam Probability: **High**

29. *Answer choices:*

(see index for correct answer)

- a. market monetarist
- b. Shadow Open Market Committee
- c. SELIC
- d. Monetary policy

Guidance: level 1

:: Competition (economics) ::

_____ arises whenever at least two parties strive for a goal which cannot be shared: where one's gain is the other's loss .

Exam Probability: **Low**

30. *Answer choices:*

(see index for correct answer)

- a. Decartelization
- b. Economic forces
- c. Leapfrogging
- d. Level playing field

Guidance: level 1

:: Mathematical and quantitative methods (economics) ::

_____ is the study of mathematical models of strategic interaction between rational decision-makers. It has applications in all fields of social science, as well as in logic and computer science. Originally, it addressed zero-sum games, in which one person's gains result in losses for the other participants. Today, _____ applies to a wide range of behavioral relations, and is now an umbrella term for the science of logical decision making in humans, animals, and computers.

Exam Probability: **Low**

31. *Answer choices:*

(see index for correct answer)

- a. Instrumental variable
- b. Supporting hyperplane
- c. Confrontation analysis
- d. Game theory

Guidance: level 1

:: Economics terminology ::

_____ is the total receipts a seller can obtain from selling goods or services to buyers. It can be written as P × Q, which is the price of the goods multiplied by the quantity of the sold goods.

Exam Probability: **Medium**

32. *Answer choices:*

(see index for correct answer)

- a. money creation
- b. Capital good
- c. Total revenue
- d. Macro risk

Guidance: level 1

:: Algebra ::

In linear algebra, the _____ is a scalar value that can be computed from the elements of a square matrix and encodes certain properties of the linear transformation described by the matrix. The _____ of a matrix A is denoted det, det A, or A. Geometrically, it can be viewed as the volume scaling factor of the linear transformation described by the matrix. This is also the signed volume of the n-dimensional parallelepiped spanned by the column or row vectors of the matrix. The _____ is positive or negative according to whether the linear mapping preserves or reverses the orientation of n-space.

33. *Answer choices:*

(see index for correct answer)

- a. Determinant
- b. monomial

Guidance: level 1

:: Keynesian economics ::

_____ are a group of various macroeconomic theories about how in the short run – and especially during recessions – economic output is strongly influenced by aggregate demand . In the Keynesian view, named for British economist John Maynard Keynes, aggregate demand does not necessarily equal the productive capacity of the economy; instead, it is influenced by a host of factors and sometimes behaves erratically, affecting production, employment, and inflation.

Exam Probability: **High**

34. *Answer choices:*

(see index for correct answer)

- a. Keynesian economics
- b. Functional finance
- c. We are all Keynesians now

- d. Underemployment equilibrium

Guidance: level 1

:: New institutional economics ::

In law and economics, the _____ describes the economic efficiency of an economic allocation or outcome in the presence of externalities. The theorem states that if trade in an externality is possible and there are sufficiently low transaction costs, bargaining will lead to a Pareto efficient outcome regardless of the initial allocation of property. In practice, obstacles to bargaining or poorly defined property rights can prevent Coasean bargaining. This "theorem" is commonly attributed to Nobel Memorial Prize in Economic Sciences winner Ronald Coase during his tenure at the London School of Economics, SUNY at Buffalo, University of Virginia, and University of Chicago.

Exam Probability: **High**

35. *Answer choices:*

(see index for correct answer)

- a. Coase theorem
- b. transaction costs

Guidance: level 1

:: United States housing bubble ::

In economics, a _____ is a business cycle contraction when there is a general decline in economic activity. Macroeconomic indicators such as GDP , investment spending, capacity utilization, household income, business profits, and inflation fall, while bankruptcies and the unemployment rate rise. In the United Kingdom, it is defined as a negative economic growth for two consecutive quarters.

Exam Probability: **High**

36. *Answer choices:*

(see index for correct answer)

- a. Community Reinvestment Act
- b. Deed in lieu of foreclosure
- c. Green shoots
- d. Predatory mortgage servicing

Guidance: level 1

:: Scarcity ::

A _____ , also known as excess burden or allocative inefficiency, is a loss of economic efficiency that can occur when the free market equilibrium for a good or a service is not achieved. That can be caused by monopoly pricing in the case of artificial scarcity, an externality, a tax or subsidy, or a binding price ceiling or price floor such as a minimum wage.

Exam Probability: **Low**

37. *Answer choices:*

(see index for correct answer)

- a. Scarcity value
- b. Deadweight loss
- c. Post-Scarcity Anarchism
- d. Excess demand

Guidance: level 1

:: Resource economics ::

A _____ is a source or supply from which a benefit is produced and it has some utility. _____ s can broadly be classified upon their availability—they are classified into renewable and non-renewable _____ s.Examples of non renewable _____ s are coal ,crude oil natural gas nuclear energy etc. Examples of renewable _____ s are air,water,wind,solar energy etc. They can also be classified as actual and potential on the basis of level of development and use, on the basis of origin they can be classified as biotic and abiotic, and on the basis of their distribution, as ubiquitous and localized . An item becomes a _____ with time and developing technology. Typically, _____ s are materials, energy, services, staff, knowledge, or other assets that are transformed to produce benefit and in the process may be consumed or made unavailable. Benefits of _____ utilization may include increased wealth, proper functioning of a system, or enhanced well-being. From a human perspective a natural _____ is anything obtained from the environment to satisfy human needs and wants. From a broader biological or ecological perspective a _____ satisfies the needs of a living organism .

Exam Probability: **Medium**

38. *Answer choices:*

(see index for correct answer)

- a. Gordon-Schaefer Model
- b. World Resources Forum
- c. Bioeconomics
- d. Resource

Guidance: level 1

:: Interest rates ::

The concept of real interest rate is useful to account for the impact of inflation. In the case of a loan, it is this real interest that the lender effectively receives. For example, if the lender is receiving 8 percent from a loan and the inflation rate is also 8 percent, then the real rate of interest is zero: despite the increased nominal amount of currency received, the lender would have no monetary value benefit from such a loan because each unit of currency would get devaluated due to inflation by the same factor as the nominal amount gets increased.

Exam Probability: **Low**

39. *Answer choices:*

(see index for correct answer)

- a. Interest rate
- b. Bank rate

- c. Nominal interest rate
- d. Overnight rate

Guidance: level 1

:: Market structure and pricing ::

_____ has historically emerged in two separate types of discussions in economics, that of Adam Smith on the one hand, and that of Karl Marx on the other hand. Adam Smith in his writing on economics stressed the importance of laissez-faire principles outlining the operation of the market in the absence of dominant political mechanisms of control, while Karl Marx discussed the working of the market in the presence of a controlled economy sometimes referred to as a command economy in the literature. Both types of _____ have been in historical evidence throughout the twentieth century and twenty-first century.

Exam Probability: **Medium**

40. *Answer choices:*

(see index for correct answer)

- a. Cellophane paradox
- b. Market structure
- c. Market concentration
- d. Megacorpstate

Guidance: level 1

:: Price controls ::

_____ are governmental restrictions on the prices that can be charged
for goods and services in a market. The intent behind implementing such
controls can stem from the desire to maintain affordability of goods even
during shortages, and to slow inflation, or, alternatively, to ensure a minimum
income for providers of certain goods or a minimum wage. There are two primary
forms of price control, a price ceiling, the maximum price that can be charged,
and a price floor, the minimum price that can be charged.

Exam Probability: **Medium**

41. *Answer choices:*

(see index for correct answer)

- a. Price controls
- b. Exchange control
- c. Edict on Maximum Prices
- d. Administered price

Guidance: level 1

:: Economics terminology ::

In economics, _____ or just capital is a factor of production , consisting of machinery, buildings, computers, and the like. The production function takes the general form Y=f, where Y is the amount of output produced, K is the amount of capital stock used, L is the amount of labor used, and N is the amount of natural resources used. In economic theory, _____ is one of the three primary factors of production; the others are natural resources , and laborthe stock of competences embodied in the labor force. _____ is distinct from human capital , circulating capital, and financial capital. _____ is fixed capital, which is any kind of real physical asset that is not used up in the production of a product. Usually the value of land is not included in _____ as it is not a reproducible product of human activities.

Exam Probability: **Medium**

42. *Answer choices:*

(see index for correct answer)

- a. Blanket order
- b. Production possibility frontier
- c. Spruce-pine-fir
- d. Capital outflow

Guidance: level 1

:: Economics terminology ::

The law or principle of _____ holds that under free trade, an agent will produce more of and consume less of a good for which they have a _____. _____ is the economic reality describing the work gains from trade for individuals, firms, or nations, which arise from differences in their factor endowments or technological progress. In an economic model, agents have a _____ over others in producing a particular good if they can produce that good at a lower relative opportunity cost or autarky price, i.e. at a lower relative marginal cost prior to trade. One shouldn't compare the monetary costs of production or even the resource costs of production. Instead, one must compare the opportunity costs of producing goods across countries.

Exam Probability: **Low**

43. *Answer choices:*

(see index for correct answer)

- a. Comparative advantage
- b. Elevator economics
- c. capital stock
- d. federal funds

Guidance: level 1

:: Microeconomics ::

In economics, _____ , resources, or inputs are what is used in the production process to produce output—that is, finished goods and services. The utilized amounts of the various inputs determine the quantity of output according to the relationship called the production function. There are three basic resources or _____ : land, labor, and capital. The factors are also frequently labeled "producer goods or services" to distinguish them from the goods or services purchased by consumers, which are frequently labeled "consumer goods".

Exam Probability: **Medium**

44. *Answer choices:*

(see index for correct answer)

- a. National Competition Policy
- b. Whitemail
- c. Factors of production
- d. Preference revelation

Guidance: level 1

:: Business terms ::

_____ are the net benefits of a corporation's operation. _____ is also the amount on which corporate tax is due. For an analysis of specific aspects of corporate operations several more specific terms are used as EBIT -- _____ before interest and taxes, EBITDA - _____ before interest, taxes, depreciation, and amortization.

45. *Answer choices:*

(see index for correct answer)

- a. Information technology outsourcing
- b. Earnings
- c. Lump sum turnkey
- d. Funding

Guidance: level 1

:: Costs ::

In economics, an _____ , also called an imputed cost, implied cost, or notional cost, is the opportunity cost equal to what a firm must give up in order to use a factor of production for which it already owns and thus does not pay rent. It is the opposite of an explicit cost, which is borne directly. In other words, an _____ is any cost that results from using an asset instead of renting it out or selling it. The term also applies to foregone income from choosing not to work.

Exam Probability: **Medium**

46. *Answer choices:*

(see index for correct answer)

- a. Cost of products sold

- b. Implicit cost
- c. Indirect costs
- d. Cost competitiveness of fuel sources

Guidance: level 1

:: Economics of uncertainty ::

_____ is the possibility of losing something of value. Values can be gained or lost when taking _____ resulting from a given action or inaction, foreseen or unforeseen . _____ can also be defined as the intentional interaction with uncertainty. Uncertainty is a potential, unpredictable, and uncontrollable outcome; _____ is a consequence of action taken in spite of uncertainty.

Exam Probability: **High**

47. *Answer choices:*
(see index for correct answer)

- a. Risk
- b. Risk inclination model
- c. state price vector
- d. Risk inclination formula

Guidance: level 1

:: Communism in Russia ::

The _____ , officially the Union of Soviet Socialist Republics , was a socialist state in Eurasia that existed from 1922 to 1991. Nominally a union of multiple national Soviet republics, its government and economy were highly centralized. The country was a one-party state, governed by the Communist Party with Moscow as its capital in its largest republic, the Russian Soviet Federative Socialist Republic . Other major urban centres were Leningrad, Kiev, Minsk, Alma-Ata, and Novosibirsk. It spanned over 10,000 kilometres east to west across 11 time zones, and over 7,200 kilometres north to south. It had five climate zones: tundra, taiga, steppes, desert and mountains.

Exam Probability: **Low**

48. *Answer choices:*

(see index for correct answer)

- a. Russian Revolution
- b. Soviet Union
- c. Russian Soviet Federative Socialist Republic

Guidance: level 1

:: Economics terminology ::

_____ , sometimes referred to as dry _____ , is the solid surface of Earth that is not permanently covered by water. The vast majority of human activity throughout history has occurred in _____ areas that support agriculture, habitat, and various natural resources. Some life forms have developed from predecessor species that lived in bodies of water.

Exam Probability: **High**

49. *Answer choices:*

(see index for correct answer)

- a. Technostructure
- b. Zerat
- c. Land
- d. Capital cost

Guidance: level 1

:: Unemployment ::

The _____ is the name that was given to a key concept in the study of economic activity. Milton Friedman and Edmund Phelps, tackling this `human` problem in the 1960s, both received the Nobel Prize in economics for their work, and the development of the concept is cited as a main motivation behind the prize. A simplistic summary of the concept is: `The _____ , when an economy is in a steady state of "full employment", is the proportion of the workforce who are unemployed`. Put another way, this concept clarifies that the economic term "full employment" does not mean "zero unemployment". It represents the hypothetical unemployment rate consistent with aggregate production being at the "long-run" level. This level is consistent with aggregate production in the absence of various temporary frictions such as incomplete price adjustment in labor and goods markets. The _____ therefore corresponds to the unemployment rate prevailing under a classical view of determination of activity.

Exam Probability: **Low**

50. *Answer choices:*
(see index for correct answer)

- a. Male unemployment
- b. Structural unemployment
- c. Mount Street Club
- d. Texas Workforce Commission

Guidance: level 1

:: Great Recession ::

The _____ was a period of general economic decline observed in world markets during the late 2000s and early 2010s. The scale and timing of the recession varied from country to country . The International Monetary Fund has concluded that it had the most severe economic and financial meltdown ever since the Great Depression and it is frequently seen as the second worst downturn of all time.

Exam Probability: **Low**

51. *Answer choices:*

(see index for correct answer)

- a. Thomas Herndon
- b. Business Consulting International
- c. The Second Great Depression
- d. Great Recession

Guidance: level 1

:: Economics curves ::

In economics, the _____ is a graphical representation of the distribution of income or of wealth. It was developed by Max O. Lorenz in 1905 for representing inequality of the wealth distribution.

Exam Probability: **Low**

52. *Answer choices:*

(see index for correct answer)

- a. Supply and demand
- b. Cost curve
- c. Beveridge curve
- d. Lorenz curve

Guidance: level 1

:: Economic policy ::

The _____ of governments covers the systems for setting levels of taxation, government budgets, the money supply and interest rates as well as the labour market, national ownership, and many other areas of government interventions into the economy.

Exam Probability: **Low**

53. *Answer choices:*

(see index for correct answer)

- a. Fiscal sustainability
- b. Local ownership import substituting
- c. Stimulus
- d. Earnings test

:: Economics terminology ::

In economics, profit in the accounting sense of the excess of revenue over cost is the sum of two components: normal profit and _____ . All understanding of profit should be broken down into three aspects: the size of profit, the portion of the total income, and the rate of profit . Normal profit is the profit that is necessary to just cover the opportunity costs of the owner-manager or of the firm's investors. In the absence of this profit, these parties would withdraw their time and funds from the firm and use them to better advantage elsewhere. In contrast, _____ , sometimes called excess profit, is profit in excess of what is required to cover the opportunity costs.

Exam Probability: **High**

54. *Answer choices:*

(see index for correct answer)

- a. Economic profit
- b. Base period
- c. Comparative advantage
- d. External cost

:: International macroeconomics ::

The balance of trade, commercial balance, or net exports , is the difference between the monetary value of a nation's exports and imports over a certain time period. Sometimes a distinction is made between a balance of trade for goods versus one for services. The balance of trade measures a flow of exports and imports over a given period of time. The notion of the balance of trade does not mean that exports and imports are "in balance" with each other.

Exam Probability: **Low**

55. *Answer choices:*

(see index for correct answer)

- a. Asset-backed commercial paper program
- b. trade surplus
- c. net export
- d. net exports

Guidance: level 1

:: Industrial organization ::

In economics, specifically general equilibrium theory, a perfect market is defined by several idealizing conditions, collectively called _____ . In theoretical models where conditions of _____ hold, it has been theoretically demonstrated that a market will reach an equilibrium in which the quantity supplied for every product or service, including labor, equals the quantity demanded at the current price. This equilibrium would be a Pareto optimum.

56. *Answer choices:*

(see index for correct answer)

- a. Path dependence
- b. Perfect competition
- c. Inside contracting
- d. Limit price

Guidance: level 1

:: World government ::

The _____ is an intergovernmental organization that is concerned with the regulation of international trade between nations. The WTO officially commenced on 1 January 1995 under the Marrakesh Agreement, signed by 124 nations on 15 April 1994, replacing the General Agreement on Tariffs and Trade , which commenced in 1948. It is the largest international economic organization in the world.

Exam Probability: **Low**

57. *Answer choices:*

(see index for correct answer)

- a. World Trade Organization
- b. International Youth Leadership Conference

- c. Globalism
- d. One World

Guidance: level 1

:: Taxation ::

A subsidy or government incentive is a form of financial aid or support extended to an economic sector generally with the aim of promoting economic and social policy. Although commonly extended from government, the term subsidy can relate to any type of support – for example from NGOs or as implicit _____ . _____ come in various forms including: direct and indirect .

Exam Probability: **Low**

58. *Answer choices:*

(see index for correct answer)

- a. Cost of goods sold
- b. Tax buoyancy
- c. Repatriation tax holiday
- d. Subsidies

Guidance: level 1

:: Economics curves ::

In microeconomics, _____ is an economic model of price determination in a market. It postulates that, holding all else equal, in a competitive market, the unit price for a particular good, or other traded item such as labor or liquid financial assets, will vary until it settles at a point where the quantity demanded will equal the quantity supplied, resulting in an economic equilibrium for price and quantity transacted.

Exam Probability: **Low**

59. *Answer choices:*

(see index for correct answer)

- a. Contract curve
- b. Kuznets curve
- c. Supply and demand
- d. Demand curve

Guidance: level 1

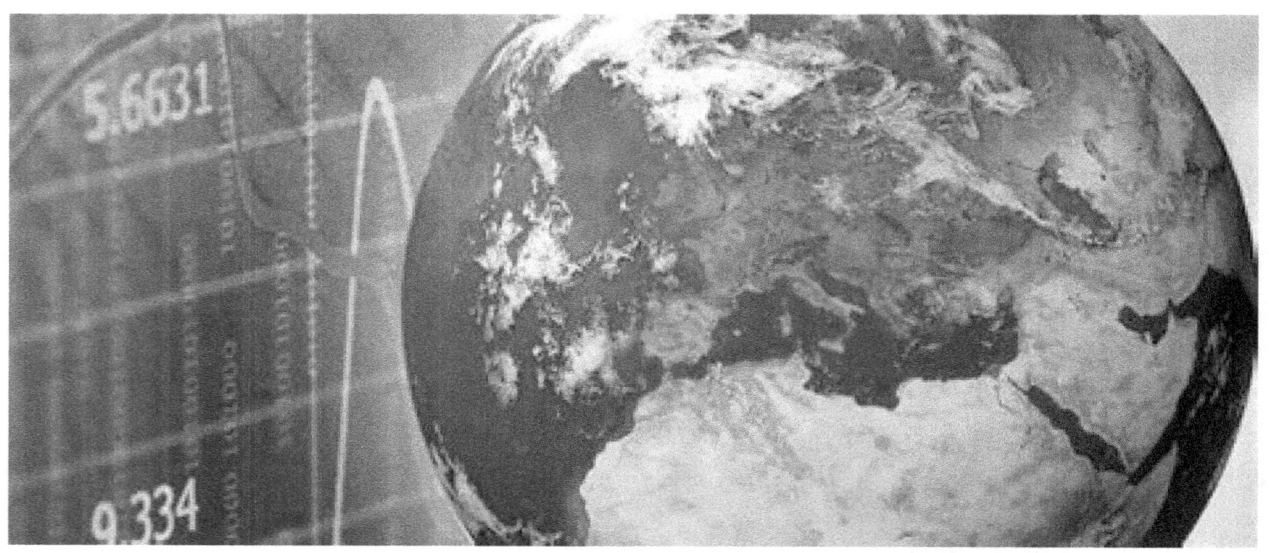

Fundamental economics

Economic analysis can be applied throughout society, in business, finance, health care, and government. Economic analysis is sometimes also applied to such diverse subjects as crime, education, the family, law, politics, religion, social institutions, war, science, and the environment.

:: Money ::

_____ is one of the three fundamental functions of money in mainstream economics. It is a widely accepted token which can be exchanged for goods and services. Because it can be exchanged for any good or service it acts as an intermediary instrument and avoids the limitations of barter; where what one wants has to be exactly matched with what the other has to offer.

Exam Probability: **Low**

1. *Answer choices:*

(see index for correct answer)

- a. Medium of exchange
- b. Chained dollars
- c. Allowance
- d. Monopoly money

Guidance: level 1

:: Economics terminology ::

A _____ is a durable good that is used in the production of goods or services. _____ s are one of the three types of producer goods, the other two being land and labour. The three are also known collectively as "primary factors of production"

Exam Probability: **Medium**

2. *Answer choices:*

(see index for correct answer)

- a. Economics of participation
- b. Capital good
- c. Consumer unit
- d. Spatial inequality

:: Goods ::

In economics, a _____ is a good that is both non-excludable and non-rivalrous in that individuals cannot be excluded from use or could be enjoyed without paying for it, and where use by one individual does not reduce availability to others or the goods can be effectively consumed simultaneously by more than one person. This is in contrast to a common good which is non-excludable but is rivalrous to a certain degree.

Exam Probability: **Medium**

3. *Answer choices:*

(see index for correct answer)

- a. Good
- b. Demerit good
- c. Yellow goods
- d. Private good

:: Scarcity ::

In economics, _____ is any payment to an owner or factor of production in excess of the costs needed to bring that factor into production. In classical economics, _____ is any payment made or benefit received for non-produced inputs such as location and for assets formed by creating official privilege over natural opportunities . In the moral economy of neoclassical economics, _____ includes income gained by labor or state beneficiaries of other "contrived" exclusivity, such as labor guilds and unofficial corruption.

Exam Probability: Low

4. Answer choices:

(see index for correct answer)

- a. Economic rent
- b. Deadweight loss
- c. Thoughts and Details on Scarcity
- d. Excess demand

Guidance: level 1

:: Economics curves ::

The _____ is a single-equation econometric model, named after WilliamPhillips, describing a historical inverse relationship between rates of unemployment and corresponding rates of rises in wages that result within an economy. Stated simply, decreased unemployment, in an economy will correlate with higher rates of wage rises. Phillips did not himself state there was any relationship between employment and inflation; this notion was a trivial deduction from his statistical findings. Samuelson and Solow made the connection explicit and subsequently Milton Friedman and Edmund Phelpsput the theoretical structure in place. In so doing, Friedman was to successfully predict the imminent collapse of Phillips' a-theoretic correlation.

Exam Probability: **Medium**

5. *Answer choices:*

(see index for correct answer)

- a. Cost curve
- b. Adaptive projected subgradient method
- c. Phillips curve
- d. Demand curve

Guidance: level 1

:: Employment compensation ::

_____ s are wages adjusted for inflation, or, equivalently, wages in terms of the amount of goods and services that can be bought. This term is used in contrast to nominal wages or unadjusted wages.

6. *Answer choices:*

(see index for correct answer)

- a. Automatic Data Processing
- b. Long service leave
- c. Real wage
- d. New York Disability Benefits Law

Guidance: level 1

:: Production economics ::

In economics long run is a theoretical concept where all markets are in equilibrium, and all prices and quantities have fully adjusted and are in equilibrium. The long run contrasts with the _____ where there are some constraints and markets are not fully in equilibrium.

Exam Probability: **Medium**

7. *Answer choices:*

(see index for correct answer)

- a. Multifactor productivity
- b. Total factor productivity
- c. Peer production

- d. Short run

Guidance: level 1

:: Financial markets ::

In economics and finance, _____ is the practice of taking advantage of a price difference between two or more markets: striking a combination of matching deals that capitalize upon the imbalance, the profit being the difference between the market prices. When used by academics, an _____ is a transaction that involves no negative cash flow at any probabilistic or temporal state and a positive cash flow in at least one state; in simple terms, it is the possibility of a risk-free profit after transaction costs. For example, an _____ opportunity is present when there is the opportunity to instantaneously buy something for a low price and sell it for a higher price.

Exam Probability: **Medium**

8. *Answer choices:*

(see index for correct answer)

- a. Industry Classification Benchmark
- b. CUSIP-linked MIP code
- c. Arbitrage
- d. Long

Guidance: level 1

:: Markets (customer bases) ::

A _____ is any systematic process enabling many market players to bid and ask: helping bidders and sellers interact and make deals. It is not just the price mechanism but the entire system of regulation, qualification, credentials, reputations and clearing that surrounds that mechanism and makes it operate in a social context.

Exam Probability: **High**

9. *Answer choices:*

(see index for correct answer)

- a. Economic equilibrium
- b. Market system
- c. Contestable market
- d. Vertical market

Guidance: level 1

:: Cambodian Civil War ::

The _____ , also known as the Second Indochina War, and in Vietnam as the Resistance War Against America or simply the American War, was an undeclared war in Vietnam, Laos, and Cambodia from 1 November 1955 to the fall of Saigon on 30 April 1975. It was the second of the Indochina Wars and was officially fought between North Vietnam and South Vietnam. North Vietnam was supported by the Soviet Union, China, and other communist allies; South Vietnam was supported by the United States, South Korea, the Philippines, Australia, Thailand and other anti-communist allies. The war is considered a Cold War-era proxy war from some US perspectives. It lasted some 19 years with direct U.S. involvement ending in 1973 following the Paris Peace Accords, and included the Laotian Civil War and the Cambodian Civil War, resulting in all three countries becoming communist states in 1975.

Exam Probability: **High**

10. *Answer choices:*

(see index for correct answer)

- a. Dien Del
- b. Vietnam War
- c. Dominique Borella
- d. Cambodian Civil War

Guidance: level 1

:: Supply chain management terms ::

Goods are items that are usually tangible, such as pens, salt, apples, and hats. Services are activities provided by other people, who include doctors, lawn care workers, dentists, barbers, waiters, or online servers, a book, a digital videogame or a digital movie. Taken together, it is the production, distribution, and consumption of _____ which underpins all economic activity and trade. According to economic theory, consumption of _____ is assumed to provide utility to the consumer or end-user, although businesses also consume _____ in the course of producing other _____ .

Exam Probability: **Low**

11. *Answer choices:*

(see index for correct answer)

- a. Economic good
- b. Certified Supply Chain Professional
- c. Goods and services
- d. Consumables

Guidance: level 1

:: Social economy ::

A _____ is a member-owned financial cooperative, controlled by its members and operated on the principle of people helping people, providing its members credit at competitive rates as well as other financial services.

Exam Probability: **Medium**

12. *Answer choices:*

(see index for correct answer)

- a. Social entrepreneurship
- b. Solidarity economy
- c. Credit union
- d. Non-profit distributing organisation

Guidance: level 1

:: Demand ::

_____ is the quantity of a good that consumers are willing and able to purchase at various prices during a given period of time.

Exam Probability: **High**

13. *Answer choices:*

(see index for correct answer)

- a. Wealth elasticity of demand
- b. price elastic
- c. Demand
- d. Demand-pull theory

Guidance: level 1

:: Foreign direct investment ::

A _____ is an investment in the form of a controlling ownership in a business in one country by an entity based in another country. It is thus distinguished from a foreign portfolio investment by a notion of direct control.

Exam Probability: **Medium**

14. *Answer choices:*

(see index for correct answer)

- a. EB-5 visa
- b. Nation branding
- c. Foreign direct investment
- d. Foreign direct investment in Iran

Guidance: level 1

:: Macroeconomic aggregates ::

In macroeconomics, _____ or Domestic Final Demand is the total demand for final goods and services in an economy at a given time. It is often called effective demand, though at other times this term is distinguished. This is the demand for the gross domestic product of a country. It specifies the amounts of goods and services that will be purchased at all possible price levels.

15. *Answer choices:*

(see index for correct answer)

- a. Aggregate expenditure
- b. aggregate supply
- c. Aggregate demand

Guidance: level 1

:: National accounts ::

A _____ is monetary compensation paid by an employer to an employee in exchange for work done. Payment may be calculated as a fixed amount for each task completed , or at an hourly or daily rate , or based on an easily measured quantity of work done.

Exam Probability: **High**

16. *Answer choices:*

(see index for correct answer)

- a. Wage
- b. Intermediate consumption
- c. Gross value added
- d. Capital formation

:: Microeconomics ::

An _____ is a contingent motivator. Traditional _____ s are extrinsic motivators which reward actions to yield a desired outcome. The effectiveness of traditional _____ s has changed as the needs of Western society have evolved. While the traditional _____ model is effective when there is a defined procedure and goal for a task, Western society started to require a higher volume of critical thinkers, so the traditional model became less effective. Institutions are now following a trend in implementing strategies that rely on intrinsic motivations rather than the extrinsic motivations that the traditional _____ s foster.

Exam Probability: **Medium**

17. *Answer choices:*

(see index for correct answer)

- a. Surface Freight Forwarder Deregulation Act of 1986
- b. Microeconomics
- c. Incentive
- d. Economic cost

:: Corporate finance ::

_____ is a form of stock which may have any combination of features not possessed by common stock including properties of both an equity and a debt instrument, and is generally considered a hybrid instrument. _____ s are senior to common stock, but subordinate to bonds in terms of claim and may have priority over common stock in the payment of dividends and upon liquidation. Terms of the _____ are described in the issuing company's articles of association or articles of incorporation.

Exam Probability: **High**

18. *Answer choices:*

(see index for correct answer)

- a. Standby Equity Distribution Agreement
- b. Cash sweep
- c. Preferred stock
- d. Capitalization table

Guidance: level 1

:: Stochastic processes ::

_____ is a system of rules that are created and enforced through social or governmental institutions to regulate behavior. It has been defined both as "the Science of Justice" and "the Art of Justice". _____ is a system that regulates and ensures that individuals or a community adhere to the will of the state. State-enforced _____ s can be made by a collective legislature or by a single legislator, resulting in statutes, by the executive through decrees and regulations, or established by judges through precedent, normally in common _____ jurisdictions. Private individuals can create legally binding contracts, including arbitration agreements that may elect to accept alternative arbitration to the normal court process. The formation of _____ s themselves may be influenced by a constitution, written or tacit, and the rights encoded therein. The _____ shapes politics, economics, history and society in various ways and serves as a mediator of relations between people.

Exam Probability: **Low**

19. *Answer choices:*

(see index for correct answer)

- a. Queueing theory
- b. Dissociated press
- c. Markov information source
- d. Jackson network

Guidance: level 1

:: New Deal ::

The _____ was a series of programs, public work projects, financial reforms, and regulations enacted by President Franklin D. Roosevelt in the United States between 1933 and 1936. It responded to needs for relief, reform, and recovery from the Great Depression. Major federal programs included the Civilian Conservation Corps , the Civil Works Administration , the Farm Security Administration , the National Industrial Recovery Act of 1933 and the Social Security Administration . They provided support for farmers, the unemployed, youth and the elderly. The _____ included new constraints and safeguards on the banking industry and efforts to re-inflate the economy after prices had fallen sharply. _____ programs included both laws passed by Congress as well as presidential executive orders during the first term of the presidency of Franklin D. Roosevelt.

Exam Probability: **Medium**

20. *Answer choices:*

(see index for correct answer)

- a. Sentinels of the Republic
- b. New Deal
- c. American Student Union
- d. National Housing Act of 1934

Guidance: level 1

:: Philosophy of science ::

A _____ is a contemplative and rational type of abstract or generalizing thinking, or the results of such thinking. Depending on the context, the results might, for example, include generalized explanations of how nature works. The word has its roots in ancient Greek, but in modern use it has taken on several related meanings.

Exam Probability: **Low**

21. *Answer choices:*

(see index for correct answer)

- a. Computational epistemology
- b. Rhetoric of science
- c. Human biocomputer
- d. Episteme

Guidance: level 1

:: Export ::

An _____ in international trade is a good or service produced in one country that is bought by someone in another country. The seller of such goods and services is an _____ er; the foreign buyer is an importer.

Exam Probability: **Medium**

22. *Answer choices:*

- a. Export hay
- b. Export
- c. Live export

Guidance: level 1

:: Feudalism ::

A _____ is an organization, usually a group of people or a company, authorized to act as a single entity and recognized as such in law. Early incorporated entities were established by charter . Most jurisdictions now allow the creation of new _____ s through registration.

Exam Probability: **Low**

23. *Answer choices:*

- a. Manorialism
- b. Mesne
- c. Precarium
- d. Corporation

Guidance: level 1

:: Crisis ::

A _____ is any event that is going to lead to an unstable and dangerous situation affecting an individual, group, community, or whole society. Crises are deemed to be negative changes in the security, economic, political, societal, or environmental affairs, especially when they occur abruptly, with little or no warning. More loosely, it is a term meaning "a testing time" or an "emergency event".

Exam Probability: **High**

24. *Answer choices:*

(see index for correct answer)

- a. Crisis
- b. Crisis theory
- c. Crisis plan
- d. Situational crisis communication theory

Guidance: level 1

:: Microeconomics ::

In financial accounting, an _____ is any resource owned by the business. Anything tangible or intangible that can be owned or controlled to produce value and that is held by a company to produce positive economic value is an _____ . Simply stated, _____ s represent value of ownership that can be converted into cash . The balance sheet of a firm records the monetary value of the _____ s owned by that firm. It covers money and other valuables belonging to an individual or to a business.

Exam Probability: **High**

25. *Answer choices:*

(see index for correct answer)

- a. Marginal revenue
- b. Price discrimination
- c. Lerner index
- d. Herfindahl index

Guidance: level 1

:: International economics ::

In finance, an _____ is the rate at which one currency will be exchanged for another. It is also regarded as the value of one country's currency in relation to another currency. For example, an interbank _____ of 114 Japanese yen to the United States dollar means that ¥114 will be exchanged for each US$1 or that US$1 will be exchanged for each ¥114. In this case it is said that the price of a dollar in relation to yen is ¥114, or equivalently that the price of a yen in relation to dollars is $1/114.

26. *Answer choices:*

(see index for correct answer)

- a. Federal Office of Economics and Export Control
- b. Spaghetti bowl effect
- c. World Bank residual model
- d. Transfer problem

Guidance: level 1

:: Stability theory ::

In numerous fields of study, the component of _____ within a system is generally characterized by some of the outputs or internal states growing without bounds. Not all systems that are not stable are unstable; systems can also be marginally stable or exhibit limit cycle behavior.

Exam Probability: **Medium**

27. *Answer choices:*

(see index for correct answer)

- a. Saddle point
- b. Instability
- c. Control-Lyapunov function

- d. Jury stability criterion

Guidance: level 1

:: International economics ::

_____ is an agreement in which one company hires another company to be responsible for a planned or existing activity that is or could be done internally.and sometimes involves transferring employees and assets from one firm to another.

Exam Probability: **High**

28. *Answer choices:*
(see index for correct answer)

- a. Outsourcing
- b. Insourcing
- c. Sourcing advisory
- d. Harberger-Laursen-Metzler effect

Guidance: level 1

:: Debt ::

A _____ is a colloquial term for the provision of financial help to a corporation or country which otherwise would be on the brink of failure or bankruptcy.

Exam Probability: **Low**

29. *Answer choices:*

(see index for correct answer)

- a. Debt-snowball method
- b. Peak debt
- c. External debt
- d. Bailout

Guidance: level 1

:: Economics ::

_____ is a situation in which the economy or an economic system could not produce any more of one good without sacrificing production of another good and without improving the production technology. In other words, _____ occurs when a good or a service is produced at the lowest possible cost. In simple terms, the concept is illustrated on a production possibility frontier , where all points on the curve are points of _____ . An equilibrium may be productively efficient without being allocatively efficient i.e. it may result in a distribution of goods where social welfare is not maximized. It is one type of economic efficiency.

30. *Answer choices:*

(see index for correct answer)

- a. Ripple effect
- b. Human rights
- c. Liquidity trap
- d. Productive efficiency

Guidance: level 1

:: Utility ::

A _____ is a form of gambling that involves the drawing of numbers at random for a prize. Lotteries are outlawed by some governments, while others endorse it to the extent of organizing a national or state _____ . It is common to find some degree of regulation of _____ by governments; the most common regulation is prohibition of sale to minors, and vendors must be licensed to sell _____ tickets. Though lotteries were common in the United States and some other countries during the 19th century, by the beginning of the 20th century, most forms of gambling, including lotteries and sweepstakes, were illegal in the U.S. and most of Europe as well as many other countries. This remained so until well after World War II. In the 1960s casinos and lotteries began to re-appear throughout the world as a means for governments to raise revenue without raising taxes.

31. *Answer choices:*

- a. Exponential utility
- b. Entropic risk measure
- c. Lottery
- d. risk-averse

Guidance: level 1

:: Communism in Russia ::

The _____ , officially the Union of Soviet Socialist Republics , was a socialist state in Eurasia that existed from 1922 to 1991. Nominally a union of multiple national Soviet republics, its government and economy were highly centralized. The country was a one-party state, governed by the Communist Party with Moscow as its capital in its largest republic, the Russian Soviet Federative Socialist Republic . Other major urban centres were Leningrad, Kiev, Minsk, Alma-Ata, and Novosibirsk. It spanned over 10,000 kilometres east to west across 11 time zones, and over 7,200 kilometres north to south. It had five climate zones: tundra, taiga, steppes, desert and mountains.

Exam Probability: **High**

32. *Answer choices:*

- a. Soviet Union
- b. Neo-Sovietism

- c. Russian Soviet Federative Socialist Republic

Guidance: level 1

:: Demand ::

_____ of demand is a measure used in economics to show the responsiveness, or elasticity, of the quantity demanded of a good or service to a change in its price when nothing but the price changes. More precisely, it gives the percentage change in quantity demanded in response to a one percent change in price.

Exam Probability: **High**

33. *Answer choices:*
(see index for correct answer)

- a. Price elasticity
- b. price elastic
- c. Wealth elasticity of demand
- d. Stock demands

Guidance: level 1

:: Outsourcing ::

_____ is the relocation of a business process from one country to another—typically an operational process, such as manufacturing, or supporting processes, such as accounting. Typically this refers to a company business, although state governments may also employ _____ . More recently, technical and administrative services have been offshored.

Exam Probability: **High**

34. *Answer choices:*

(see index for correct answer)

- a. Offshoring
- b. Service-level agreement
- c. IQor
- d. Virtual Staff Finder

Guidance: level 1

:: Economic indicators ::

The gross national income , previously known as _____ , is the total domestic and foreign output claimed by residents of a country, consisting of gross domestic product , plus factor incomes earned by foreign residents, minus income earned in the domestic economy by nonresidents . Comparing GNI to GDP shows the degree to which a nation's GDP represents domestic or international activity. GNI has gradually replaced GNP in international statistics. While being conceptually identical, it is calculated differently. GNI is the basis of calculation of the largest part of contributions to the budget of the European Union. In February 2017, Ireland's GDP became so distorted from the base erosion and profit shifting tax planning tools of U.S. multinationals, that the Central Bank of Ireland replaced Irish GDP with a new metric, Irish Modified GNI*. In 2017, Irish GDP was 162% of Irish Modified GNI*.

Exam Probability: **Medium**

35. *Answer choices:*

(see index for correct answer)

- a. University of Michigan Consumer Sentiment Index
- b. Gross national product
- c. Conference Board Leading Economic Index
- d. Travelex Confidence Index

Guidance: level 1

:: World economy ::

The _____ or global economy is the economy of the humans of the world, considered as the international exchange of goods and services that is expressed in monetary units of account. In some contexts, the two terms are distinct "international" or "global economy" being measured separately and distinguished from national economies while the " _____ " is simply an aggregate of the separate countries` measurements. Beyond the minimum standard concerning value in production, use and exchange the definitions, representations, models and valuations of the _____ vary widely. It is inseparable from the geography and ecology of Earth.

Exam Probability: **High**

36. *Answer choices:*

(see index for correct answer)

- a. World economy
- b. The World Economy

Guidance: level 1

:: Keynesian economics ::

_____ are a group of various macroeconomic theories about how in the short run – and especially during recessions – economic output is strongly influenced by aggregate demand . In the Keynesian view, named for British economist John Maynard Keynes, aggregate demand does not necessarily equal the productive capacity of the economy; instead, it is influenced by a host of factors and sometimes behaves erratically, affecting production, employment, and inflation.

37. *Answer choices:*

(see index for correct answer)

- a. Paradox of flexibility
- b. Birmingham School
- c. Keynesian economics
- d. Neoclassical synthesis

Guidance: level 1

:: Economic efficiency ::

The term _____ generally refers to an absence of efficiency. It has several meanings depending on the context in which it is used.

Exam Probability: **Medium**

38. *Answer choices:*

(see index for correct answer)

- a. Memo motion
- b. American Information Exchange
- c. economic efficiency
- d. Inefficiency

:: Taxation and efficiency ::

_____ is a macroeconomic theory arguing that economic growth can be most effectively created by lowering taxes and decreasing regulation, by which it is directly opposed to demand-side economics. According to _____, consumers will then benefit from a greater supply of goods and services at lower prices and employment will increase.

Exam Probability: **High**

39. *Answer choices:*

(see index for correct answer)

- a. Capital flight
- b. Supply-side economics
- c. supply-side
- d. Tax avoidance

:: Macroeconomics ::

_____ is a branch of economics dealing with the performance, structure, behavior, and decision-making of an economy as a whole. This includes regional, national, and global economies. Macroeconomists study aggregated indicators such as GDP, unemployment rates, national income, price indices, and the interrelations among the different sectors of the economy to better understand how the whole economy functions. They also develop models that explain the relationship between such factors as national income, output, consumption, unemployment, inflation, saving, investment, international trade, and international finance.

Exam Probability: **Low**

40. *Answer choices:*

(see index for correct answer)

- a. loanable funds market
- b. SIMIC
- c. Macroeconomics
- d. Microsimulation

Guidance: level 1

:: Federal Reserve Banks ::

A _____ is a regional bank of the Federal Reserve System, the central banking system of the United States. There are twelve in total, one for each of the twelve Federal Reserve Districts that were created by the Federal Reserve Act of 1913. The banks are jointly responsible for implementing the monetary policy set forth by the Federal Open Market Committee, and are divided as follows.

Exam Probability: **Low**

41. *Answer choices:*

(see index for correct answer)

- a. Federal Reserve Bank
- b. Federal Reserve Bank of Atlanta
- c. Federal Reserve Bank of Chicago Detroit Branch
- d. Federal Reserve Bank of Richmond

Guidance: level 1

:: Monetary economics ::

_____ are a commercial bank's holdings of deposits in accounts with a central bank , plus currency that is physically held in the bank's vault . Some central banks set minimum reserve requirements, which require banks to hold deposits at the central bank equivalent to at least a specified percentage of their liabilities such as customer deposits. Even when there are no reserve requirements, banks often opt to hold some reserves—called desired reserves—against unexpected events such as unusually large net withdrawals by customers or bank runs.

42. *Answer choices:*

(see index for correct answer)

- a. Circular cumulative causation
- b. Bank reserves
- c. Price level
- d. Asset price channel

Guidance: level 1

:: Operations research ::

_____ or stock is the goods and materials that a business holds for the ultimate goal of resale .

Exam Probability: **Low**

43. *Answer choices:*

(see index for correct answer)

- a. Carrying cost
- b. Least-cost planning methodology
- c. Operations and technology management
- d. Inventory

:: Central banks ::

A _____ , reserve bank, or monetary authority is the institution that manages the currency, money supply, and interest rates of a state or formal monetary union, and oversees their commercial banking system. In contrast to a commercial bank, a _____ possesses a monopoly on increasing the monetary base in the state, and also generally controls the printing/coining of the national currency, which serves as the state's legal tender. A _____ also acts as a lender of last resort to the banking sector during times of financial crisis. Most _____ s also have supervisory and regulatory powers to ensure the solvency of member institutions, to prevent bank runs, and to discourage reckless or fraudulent behavior by member banks.

Exam Probability: **High**

44. *Answer choices:*

(see index for correct answer)

- a. Central bank
- b. Central Bank of the Republic of Guinea
- c. Bank of Sudan
- d. Bank of Algeria

:: Standard of living ::

An individual's or a socioeconomic class's _____ is the level of wealth, comfort, material goods, and necessities available to them in a certain geographic area, usually a country. The _____ includes factors such as income, quality and availability of employment, class disparity, poverty rate, quality and affordability of housing, hours of work required to purchase necessities, gross domestic product, inflation rate, amount of leisure time every year, affordable access to quality healthcare, quality and availability of education, life expectancy, incidence of disease, cost of goods and services, infrastructure, national economic growth, economic and political stability, freedom, environmental quality, climate and safety. The _____ is closely related to quality of life.

Exam Probability: **Low**

45. *Answer choices:*

(see index for correct answer)

- a. Standard of living
- b. Standard of living in the United States
- c. Standard of living in Japan
- d. Right to an adequate standard of living

Guidance: level 1

:: Socioeconomics ::

_____ is the amount of goods and services that can be purchased with a unit of currency. For example, if one had taken one unit of currency to a store in the 1950s, it would have been possible to buy a greater number of items than would be the case today, indicating that the currency had a greater _____ in the 1950s. Currency can be either a commodity money, like gold or silver, or fiat money emitted by government sanctioned agencies.

Exam Probability: **High**

46. *Answer choices:*

(see index for correct answer)

- a. Consumerism and longevity
- b. Mandatory tipping
- c. Convergence clubs
- d. Community health

Guidance: level 1

:: Accounting terminology ::

In financial accounting, a _____ or statement of financial position or statement of financial condition is a summary of the financial balances of an individual or organization, whether it be a sole proprietorship, a business partnership, a corporation, private limited company or other organization such as Government or not-for-profit entity. Assets, liabilities and ownership equity are listed as of a specific date, such as the end of its financial year. A _____ is often described as a "snapshot of a company`s financial condition". Of the four basic financial statements, the _____ is the only statement which applies to a single point in time of a business` calendar year.

Exam Probability: **Low**

47. *Answer choices:*

(see index for correct answer)

- a. Balance sheet
- b. Checkoff
- c. Accounts payable
- d. Accounting equation

Guidance: level 1

:: Labor economics ::

_____ is a situation in which everyone who wants a job can have work hours they need on "fair wages". Because people switch jobs, _____ involves a positive stable rate of unemployment. An economy with _____ might still have underemployment where part-time workers cannot find jobs appropriate to their skill level. In macroeconomics, _____ is sometimes defined as the level of employment at which there is no cyclical or deficient-demand unemployment.

Exam Probability: **Low**

48. *Answer choices:*

(see index for correct answer)

- a. Ethnic penalty
- b. Economic activity rate
- c. Internal labor market
- d. Full employment

Guidance: level 1

:: Market structure and pricing ::

_____ is a type of imperfect competition such that many producers sell products that are differentiated from one another and hence are not perfect substitutes. In _____ , a firm takes the prices charged by its rivals as given and ignores the impact of its own prices on the prices of other firms. In the presence of coercive government, _____ will fall into government-granted monopoly. Unlike perfect competition, the firm maintains spare capacity. Models of _____ are often used to model industries. Textbook examples of industries with market structures similar to _____ include restaurants, cereal, clothing, shoes, and service industries in large cities. The "founding father" of the theory of _____ is Edward Hastings Chamberlin, who wrote a pioneering book on the subject, Theory of _____ . Joan Robinson published a book The Economics of Imperfect Competition with a comparable theme of distinguishing perfect from imperfect competition.

Exam Probability: **Medium**

49. *Answer choices:*

(see index for correct answer)

- a. Megacorpstate
- b. Cellophane paradox
- c. Market share
- d. Liberalization

Guidance: level 1

:: Costs ::

An _____ is a direct payment made to others in the course of running a business, such as wage, rent and materials, as opposed to implicit costs,land lassanare those where no actual payment is made. It is possible still to underestimate these costs, however: for example, pension contributions and other "perks" must be taken into account when considering the cost of labour.

Exam Probability: **Medium**

50. *Answer choices:*

(see index for correct answer)

- a. Business mileage reimbursement rate
- b. Explicit cost
- c. Travel and subsistence
- d. Semi-variable cost

Guidance: level 1

:: Stock market ::

_____ is freedom from, or resilience against, potential harm caused by others. Beneficiaries of _____ may be of persons and social groups, objects and institutions, ecosystems or any other entity or phenomenon vulnerable to unwanted change by its environment.

Exam Probability: **Low**

51. *Answer choices:*

(see index for correct answer)

- a. Security
- b. CNBC Ticker
- c. Slippage
- d. Swing trading

Guidance: level 1

:: Macroeconomic aggregates ::

In economics, _____ is a measure of national income. _____ is defined as the current value of all the finished goods and services in the economy. The _____ is thus the sum total of all the expenditures undertaken in the economy by the factors during a given time period. It is the expenditure incurred on consumer goods, planned investment and the expenditure made by the government in the economy. In an open economy scenario, _____ also includes the difference between the exports and the imports.

Exam Probability: **Low**

52. *Answer choices:*

(see index for correct answer)

- a. aggregate supply
- b. Aggregate expenditure
- c. Aggregate behavior

:: Financial crises ::

A _____ is any of a broad variety of situations in which some financial assets suddenly lose a large part of their nominal value. In the 19th and early 20th centuries, many financial crises were associated with banking panics, and many recessions coincided with these panics. Other situations that are often called financial crises include stock market crashes and the bursting of other financial bubbles, currency crises, and sovereign defaults. Financial crises directly result in a loss of paper wealth but do not necessarily result in significant changes in the real economy .

Exam Probability: **High**

53. *Answer choices:*

(see index for correct answer)

- a. Finnish banking crisis of 1990s
- b. Financial crisis
- c. Panic of 1825
- d. Black Monday

:: Economic systems ::

An _____ is a system of production, resource allocation and distribution of goods and services within a society or a given geographic area. It includes the combination of the various institutions, agencies, entities, decision-making processes and patterns of consumption that comprise the economic structure of a given community. As such, an _____ is a type of social system. The mode of production is a related concept. All _____ s have three basic questions to ask: what to produce, how to produce and in what quantities and who receives the output of production.

Exam Probability: **High**

54. *Answer choices:*

(see index for correct answer)

- a. Digital economy
- b. Folkhemmet
- c. Economic system
- d. Natural economy

Guidance: level 1

:: Costs ::

_____ s are costs that change as the quantity of the good or service that a business produces changes. _____ s are the sum of marginal costs over all units produced. They can also be considered normal costs. Fixed costs and _____ s make up the two components of total cost. Direct costs are costs that can easily be associated with a particular cost object. However, not all _____ s are direct costs. For example, variable manufacturing overhead costs are _____ s that are indirect costs, not direct costs. _____ s are sometimes called unit-level costs as they vary with the number of units produced.

Exam Probability: **Medium**

55. *Answer choices:*

(see index for correct answer)

- a. Variable cost
- b. Cost competitiveness of fuel sources
- c. Manufacturing cost
- d. Cost externalizing

Guidance: level 1

:: Microeconomics ::

A _____ is the price of a commodity such as a good or service in terms of another; i.e., the ratio of two prices. A _____ may be expressed in terms of a ratio between the prices of any two goods or the ratio between the price of one good and the price of a market basket of goods . A _____ is an opportunity cost. Microeconomics can be seen as the study of how economic agents react to changes in _____ s, and of how _____ s are affected by the behavior of those agents.

Exam Probability: **Low**

56. *Answer choices:*

(see index for correct answer)

- a. Relative price
- b. Yield management
- c. Price signal
- d. Shutdown

Guidance: level 1

:: Capitalism ::

A _____ , equity market or share market is the aggregation of buyers and sellers of stocks , which represent ownership claims on businesses; these may include securities listed on a public stock exchange, as well as stock that is only traded privately. Examples of the latter include shares of private companies which are sold to investors through equity crowdfunding platforms. Stock exchanges list shares of common equity as well as other security types, e.g. corporate bonds and convertible bonds.

57. *Answer choices:*

(see index for correct answer)

- a. Capitalist realism
- b. Crony-capitalism index
- c. Peak capitalism
- d. Empowerment Experiment

Guidance: level 1

:: Public choice theory ::

_____ theory is "the use of economic tools to deal with traditional problems of political science". Its content includes the study of political behavior. In political science, it is the subset of positive political theory that studies self-interested agents and their interactions, which can be represented in a number of ways – using standard constrained utility maximization, game theory, or decision theory.

58. *Answer choices:*

(see index for correct answer)

- a. Privilege
- b. Public choice

- c. Bundling
- d. Crony capitalism

Guidance: level 1

:: Monetary policy ::

_____ is the process by which the monetary authority of a country, typically the central bank or currency board, controls either the cost of very short-term borrowing or the money supply, often targeting inflation rate or interest rate to ensure price stability and general trust in the currency.

Exam Probability: **High**

59. *Answer choices:*

(see index for correct answer)

- a. Liquidity adjustment facility
- b. Money multiplier
- c. Monetary policy
- d. inflationary

Guidance: level 1

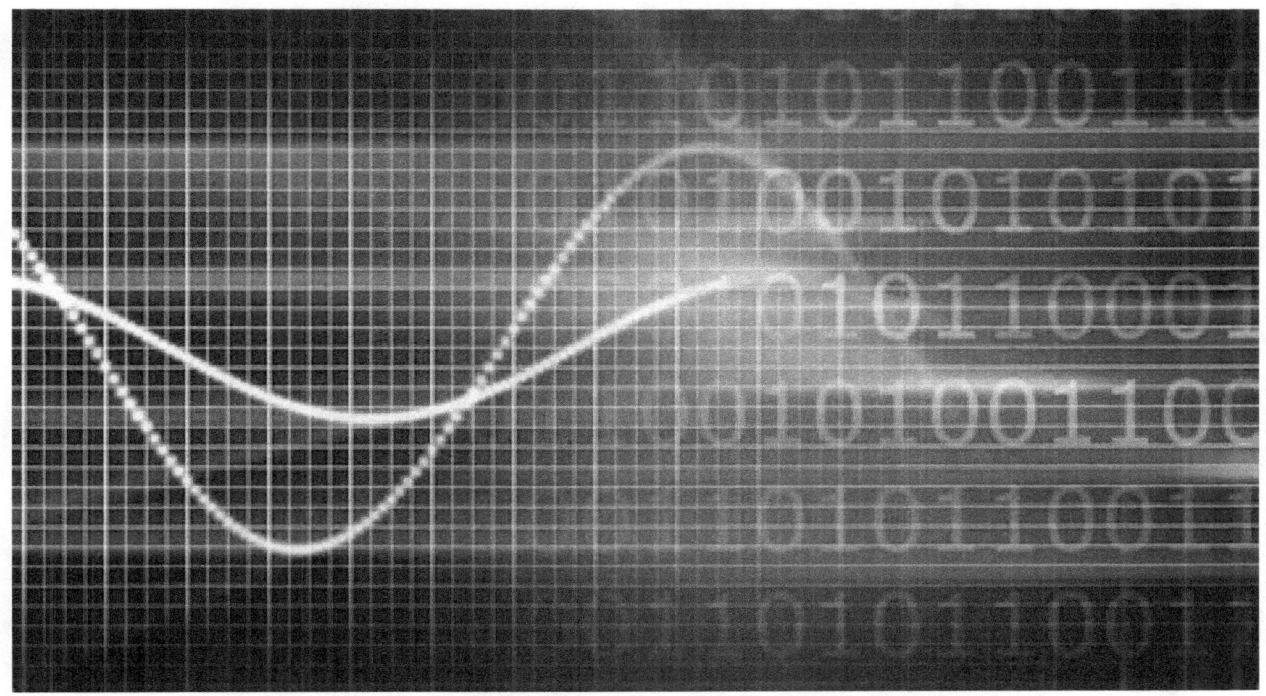

Mathematical and quantitative methods

Mathematical economics is the application of mathematical methods to represent theories and analyze problems in economics. By convention, these applied methods are beyond simple geometry, such as differential and integral calculus, difference and differential equations, matrix algebra, mathematical programming, and other computational methods.

:: Sampling (statistics) ::

In statistics, _____ is incurred when the statistical characteristics of a population are estimated from a subset, or sample, of that population. Since the sample does not include all members of the population, statistics on the sample, such as means and quartiles, generally differ from the characteristics of the entire population, which are known as parameters. For example, if one measures the height of a thousand individuals from a country of one million, the average height of the thousand is typically not the same as the average height of all one million people in the country. Since sampling is typically done to determine the characteristics of a whole population, the difference between the sample and population values is considered an error. Exact measurement of _____ is generally not feasible since the true population values are unknown.

Exam Probability: **High**

1. *Answer choices:*

(see index for correct answer)

- a. Sampling design
- b. Acquiescence bias
- c. sample size
- d. Sampling error

Guidance: level 1

:: Statistical models ::

A _____ is a type of mathematical model that is applied to the study of population dynamics.

2. *Answer choices:*

(see index for correct answer)

- a. Parametric model
- b. Latent variable model
- c. Sdc verifier
- d. Population model

Guidance: level 1

:: Design of experiments ::

In inferential statistics, the _____ is a general statement or default position that there is no relationship between two measured phenomena, or no association among groups. Testing the _____ —and thus concluding that there are or are not grounds for believing that there is a relationship between two phenomena —is a central task in the modern practice of science; the field of statistics gives precise criteria for rejecting a _____ .

3. *Answer choices:*

(see index for correct answer)

- a. Minimisation
- b. Analysis of variance

- c. Null hypothesis
- d. Repeated measures design

Guidance: level 1

:: Regression analysis ::

In statistics, _____ is a phenomenon in which one predictor variable in a multiple regression model can be linearly predicted from the others with a substantial degree of accuracy. In this situation the coefficient estimates of the multiple regression may change erratically in response to small changes in the model or the data. _____ does not reduce the predictive power or reliability of the model as a whole, at least within the sample data set; it only affects calculations regarding individual predictors. That is, a multivariate regression model with collinear predictors can indicate how well the entire bundle of predictors predicts the outcome variable, but it may not give valid results about any individual predictor, or about which predictors are redundant with respect to others.

Exam Probability: **Medium**

4. *Answer choices:*

(see index for correct answer)

- a. Multicollinearity
- b. Omitted-variable bias
- c. Regression toward the mean
- d. Partial least squares regression

:: Summary statistics ::

A _____ is a type of quantile. The first _____ is defined as the middle number between the smallest number and the median of the data set. The second _____ is the median of the data. The third _____ is the middle value between the median and the highest value of the data set.

Exam Probability: **Low**

5. *Answer choices:*

(see index for correct answer)

- a. Quartile
- b. Weighted mean
- c. Pseudomedian
- d. Hoover index

:: Price indices ::

A _____ measures changes in the price level of market basket of consumer goods and services purchased by households.

6. *Answer choices:*

(see index for correct answer)

- a. United States Chained Consumer Price Index
- b. Producer Price Index
- c. Consumer price index
- d. Average Earnings Index

Guidance: level 1

:: Time series analysis ::

A _____ is a type of statistical hypothesis test in which the null hypothesis is well specified, but the alternative hypothesis is more loosely specified. Tests constructed in this context can have the property of being at least moderately powerful against a wide range of departures from the null hypothesis. Thus, in applied statistics, a _____ provides a reasonable way of proceeding as a general check of a model's match to a dataset where there are many different ways in which the model may depart from the underlying data generating process. Use of such tests avoids having to be very specific about the particular type of departure being tested.

7. *Answer choices:*

(see index for correct answer)

- a. Wiener filter
- b. Unit root test
- c. Approximate entropy
- d. Portmanteau test

Guidance: level 1

:: Microeconomics ::

In economics, _____ is the change in the total cost that arises when the quantity produced is incremented by one unit; that is, it is the cost of producing one more unit of a good. Intuitively, _____ at each level of production includes the cost of any additional inputs required to produce the next unit. At each level of production and time period being considered, _____ s include all costs that vary with the level of production, whereas other costs that do not vary with production are fixed and thus have no _____ . For example, the _____ of producing an automobile will generally include the costs of labor and parts needed for the additional automobile but not the fixed costs of the factory that have already been incurred. In practice, marginal analysis is segregated into short and long-run cases, so that, over the long run, all costs become marginal. Where there are economies of scale, prices set at _____ will fail to cover total costs, thus requiring a subsidy. _____ pricing is not a matter of merely lowering the general level of prices with the aid of a subsidy; with or without subsidy it calls for a drastic restructuring of pricing practices, with opportunities for very substantial improvements in efficiency at critical points.

Exam Probability: **Low**

8. *Answer choices:*

(see index for correct answer)

- a. Loyalty program
- b. producer surplus
- c. Returns to scale
- d. Comparative statics

Guidance: level 1

:: Mathematical and quantitative methods (economics) ::

_____ is a method to achieve the best outcome in a mathematical model whose requirements are represented by linear relationships. _____ is a special case of mathematical programming .

Exam Probability: **Low**

9. *Answer choices:*

(see index for correct answer)

- a. Seemingly unrelated regressions
- b. Heteroscedasticity-consistent standard errors
- c. Linear programming
- d. Identity line

Guidance: level 1

:: Philosophy of science ::

An _____ definition is the articulation of _____ ization used in defining the terms of a process needed to determine the nature of an item or phenomenon and its properties such as duration, quantity, extension in space, chemical composition, etc. Since the degree of _____ ization can vary itself, it can result in a more or less _____ definition. The procedures included in definitions should be repeatable by anyone or at least by peers.

Exam Probability: **Low**

10. *Answer choices:*

(see index for correct answer)

- a. Operational
- b. Eyewitness testimony
- c. Free parameter
- d. Philosophy of chemistry

Guidance: level 1

:: Statistical charts and diagrams ::

In science and engineering, a _____ graph or _____ plot is a way of visualizing data that are related according to an exponential relationship. One axis is plotted on a logarithmic scale.

11. *Answer choices:*

(see index for correct answer)

- a. Semi-log
- b. Dual-flashlight plot
- c. Lexis diagram
- d. Control chart

Guidance: level 1

:: Statistical deviation and dispersion ::

In probability theory and statistics, _____ is a measure of the "tailedness" of the probability distribution of a real-valued random variable. In a similar way to the concept of skewness, _____ is a descriptor of the shape of a probability distribution and, just as for skewness, there are different ways of quantifying it for a theoretical distribution and corresponding ways of estimating it from a sample from a population. Depending on the particular measure of _____ that is used, there are various interpretations of _____ , and of how particular measures should be interpreted.

12. *Answer choices:*

(see index for correct answer)

- a. Standardized moment
- b. Greenwood statistic
- c. Root mean square
- d. Qualitative variation

Guidance: level 1

:: Statistical inference ::

_____ is the process of using data analysis to deduce properties of an underlying probability distribution. Inferential statistical analysis infers properties of a population, for example by testing hypotheses and deriving estimates. It is assumed that the observed data set is sampled from a larger population.

Exam Probability: **Medium**

13. *Answer choices:*

(see index for correct answer)

- a. Statistical inference
- b. Confidence region
- c. Interval estimation
- d. Bayesian inference

Guidance: level 1

:: Mathematical and quantitative methods (economics) ::

_____ is the application of statistical methods to economic data in order to give empirical content to economic relationships. More precisely, it is "the quantitative analysis of actual economic phenomena based on the concurrent development of theory and observation, related by appropriate methods of inference". An introductory economics textbook describes _____ as allowing economists "to sift through mountains of data to extract simple relationships". The first known use of the term "_____" was by Polish economist Pawel Ciompa in 1910. Jan Tinbergen is considered by many to be one of the founding fathers of _____ . Ragnar Frisch is credited with coining the term in the sense in which it is used today.

Exam Probability: **Medium**

14. *Answer choices:*

(see index for correct answer)

- a. Econometrics
- b. Fixed-point theorems in infinite-dimensional spaces
- c. Lagrange multiplier
- d. Criticisms of econometrics

Guidance: level 1

:: Econometrics ::

A _____ often refers to a set of documented requirements to be satisfied by a material, design, product, or service. A _____ is often a type of technical standard.

Exam Probability: **Medium**

15. *Answer choices:*

(see index for correct answer)

- a. Event study
- b. Specification
- c. Regression discontinuity design
- d. Heteroscedasticity

Guidance: level 1

:: Bayesian statistics ::

In Bayesian statistics, the _____ of a random event or an uncertain proposition is the conditional probability that is assigned after the relevant evidence or background is taken into account. Similarly, the _____ distribution is the probability distribution of an unknown quantity, treated as a random variable, conditional on the evidence obtained from an experiment or survey. "Posterior", in this context, means after taking into account the relevant evidence related to the particular case being examined. For instance, there is a probability of a person finding buried treasure if they dig in a random spot, and a _____ of finding buried treasure if they dig in a spot where their metal detector rings.

16. *Answer choices:*

(see index for correct answer)

- a. Variational Bayesian methods
- b. Bayesian programming
- c. Bayesian search theory
- d. Speed prior

Guidance: level 1

:: Financial data analysis ::

_____ comprises the strategies and technologies used by enterprises for the data analysis of business information. BI technologies provide historical, current and predictive views of business operations. Common functions of _____ technologies include reporting, online analytical processing, analytics, data mining, process mining, complex event processing, business performance management, benchmarking, text mining, predictive analytics and prescriptive analytics. BI technologies can handle large amounts of structured and sometimes unstructured data to help identify, develop and otherwise create new strategic business opportunities. They aim to allow for the easy interpretation of these big data. Identifying new opportunities and implementing an effective strategy based on insights can provide businesses with a competitive market advantage and long-term stability.

Exam Probability: **Medium**

17. *Answer choices:*

- a. Gross merchandise volume
- b. Reactive business intelligence
- c. Brainware
- d. Analytics

Guidance: level 1

:: Game theory ::

In game theory, _____ is a solution concept. The general idea is to provide the weakest constraints on players while still requiring that players are rational and this rationality is common knowledge among the players. It is more permissive than Nash equilibrium. Both require that players respond optimally to some belief about their opponents' actions, but Nash equilibrium requires that these beliefs be correct while _____ does not. _____ was first defined, independently, by Bernheim and Pearce .

Exam Probability: **High**

18. *Answer choices:*

- a. Complete mixing
- b. Self-confirming equilibrium
- c. Bandwidth-sharing game

- d. Evolutionarily stable strategy

Guidance: level 1

:: Analysis of variance ::

In statistics, the _____ is an extension of the one-way ANOVA that examines the influence of two different categorical independent variables on one continuous dependent variable. The two-way ANOVA not only aims at assessing the main effect of each independent variable but also if there is any interaction between them.

Exam Probability: **Medium**

19. *Answer choices:*

(see index for correct answer)

- a. Main effect
- b. Standardized mean of a contrast variable
- c. Mixed-design analysis of variance
- d. random effect

Guidance: level 1

:: Statistical tests ::

In statistics, _____ is a technique that can be used to compare means of two or more samples . This technique can be used only for numerical response data, the "Y", usually one variable, and numerical or categorical input data, the "X", always one variable, hence "one-way".

Exam Probability: **High**

20. *Answer choices:*

(see index for correct answer)

- a. G-test
- b. One-way analysis of variance
- c. P-rep
- d. Q-statistic

Guidance: level 1

:: Summary statistics ::

The _____ is a set of descriptive statistics that provide information about a dataset. It consists of the five most important sample percentiles.

Exam Probability: **Low**

21. *Answer choices:*

(see index for correct answer)

- a. Average
- b. Polychoric correlation
- c. Five-number summary
- d. Quantile

Guidance: level 1

:: Time series models ::

In statistics, econometrics and signal processing, an autoregressive model is a representation of a type of random process; as such, it is used to describe certain time-varying processes in nature, economics, etc. The _____ specifies that the output variable depends linearly on its own previous values and on a stochastic term ; thus the model is in the form of a stochastic difference equation. In machine learning, an _____ learns from a series of timed steps and takes measurements from previous actions as inputs for a regression model, in order to predict the value of the next time step.

Exam Probability: **High**

22. *Answer choices:*

(see index for correct answer)

- a. Error correction model
- b. Autoregressive model
- c. Additive white Gaussian noise
- d. Autoregressive integrated moving average

:: Statistical charts and diagrams ::

A _____ is a type of plot or mathematical diagram using Cartesian coordinates to display values for typically two variables for a set of data. If the points are coded , one additional variable can be displayed.The data are displayed as a collection of points, each having the value of one variable determining the position on the horizontal axis and the value of the other variable determining the position on the vertical axis.

Exam Probability: **Low**

23. *Answer choices:*

(see index for correct answer)

- a. Forest plot
- b. Carpet plot
- c. Statistical graphics
- d. Scatter plot

:: Computational statistics ::

In probability theory, a _____ is an adjustment that is made when a discrete distribution is approximated by a continuous distribution.

24. *Answer choices:*

(see index for correct answer)

- a. Particle filter
- b. Continuity correction
- c. Computational statistics
- d. Auxiliary particle filter

Guidance: level 1

:: Statistical terminology ::

In many scientific fields, the _____ of a system is the number of parameters of the system that may vary independently. For example, a point in the plane has two _____ for translation: its two coordinates; a non-infinitesimal object on the plane might have additional _____ s related to its orientation.

25. *Answer choices:*

(see index for correct answer)

- a. Permutation test
- b. Percentile rank
- c. Degrees of freedom
- d. Pooled variance

Guidance: level 1

:: Statistical charts and diagrams ::

A _____ is an accurate representation of the distribution of numerical data. It is an estimate of the probability distribution of a continuous variable and was first introduced by Karl Pearson. It differs from a bar graph, in the sense that a bar graph relates two variables, but a _____ relates only one. To construct a _____ , the first step is to "bin" the range of values—that is, divide the entire range of values into a series of intervals—and then count how many values fall into each interval. The bins are usually specified as consecutive, non-overlapping intervals of a variable. The bins must be adjacent, and are often of equal size.

Exam Probability: **Medium**

26. *Answer choices:*

(see index for correct answer)

- a. Histogram
- b. Fan chart
- c. Pie chart
- d. Dot plot

:: Statistical software ::

_____ is a statistics package developed at the Pennsylvania State University by researchers Barbara F. Ryan, Thomas A. Ryan, Jr., and Brian L. Joiner in 1972. It began as a light version of OMNITAB 80, a statistical analysis program by NIST. Statistical analysis software such as _____ automates calculations and the creation of graphs, allowing the user to focus more on the analysis of data and the interpretation of results. It is compatible with other _____ , Inc. software.

Exam Probability: **Low**

27. *Answer choices:*

(see index for correct answer)

- a. PSPP
- b. Minitab
- c. Epidata
- d. Statistical Solutions

:: Time series analysis ::

A _____ is a series of data points indexed in time order. Most commonly, a _____ is a sequence taken at successive equally spaced points in time. Thus it is a sequence of discrete-time data. Examples of _____ are heights of ocean tides, counts of sunspots, and the daily closing value of the Dow Jones Industrial Average.

Exam Probability: **Medium**

28. *Answer choices:*

(see index for correct answer)

- a. Time series
- b. Linear prediction
- c. Approximate entropy
- d. Structural break

Guidance: level 1

:: Statistical charts and diagrams ::

A _____ or bar graph is a chart or graph that presents categorical data with rectangular bars with heights or lengths proportional to the values that they represent. The bars can be plotted vertically or horizontally. A vertical _____ is sometimes called a line graph.

Exam Probability: **High**

29. *Answer choices:*

(see index for correct answer)

- a. X-bar chart
- b. Western Electric rules
- c. Bar chart
- d. Pie chart

Guidance: level 1

:: Price indices ::

Its importance is being undermined by the steady decline in manufactured goods as a share of spending.

Exam Probability: **High**

30. *Answer choices:*

(see index for correct answer)

- a. Producer price index
- b. Price index
- c. United States Chained Consumer Price Index
- d. RPIX

Guidance: level 1

:: Regression analysis ::

In statistics and econometrics, the _____ model is a generalization of the probit model used when there are several possible categories that the dependent variable can fall into. As such, it is an alternative to the multinomial logit model as one method of multiclass classification. It is not to be confused with the multivariate probit model, which is used to model correlated binary outcomes for more than one independent variable.

Exam Probability: **Low**

31. *Answer choices:*

(see index for correct answer)

- a. Local regression
- b. Proportional hazards model
- c. Total sum of squares
- d. Canonical analysis

Guidance: level 1

:: Chess theory ::

In trigonometry and geometry, _____ is the process of determining the location of a point by forming triangles to it from known points.

32. *Answer choices:*

(see index for correct answer)

- a. Triangulation
- b. Key square
- c. Rook and pawn versus rook endgame
- d. Chess endgame literature

Guidance: level 1

:: Regression analysis ::

In statistics, _____ measures the proportion to which a mathematical model accounts for the variation of a given data set. Often, variation is quantified as variance; then, the more specific term explained variance can be used.

33. *Answer choices:*

(see index for correct answer)

- a. Proper linear model
- b. Explained variation
- c. Overfitting

- d. Total sum of squares

Guidance: level 1

:: Behavioral finance ::

The _____ is a hypothesis that there is a seasonal anomaly in the financial market where securities' prices increase in the month of January more than in any other month. This calendar effect would create an opportunity for investors to buy stocks for lower prices before January and sell them after their value increases. As with all calendar effects, if true, it would suggest that the market is not efficient, as market efficiency would suggest that this effect should disappear.

Exam Probability: **High**

34. *Answer choices:*

(see index for correct answer)

- a. Keynesian beauty contest
- b. Disposition effect
- c. Market anomaly
- d. January effect

Guidance: level 1

:: Regression analysis ::

_____ , also known as serial correlation, is the correlation of a signal with a delayed copy of itself as a function of delay. Informally, it is the similarity between observations as a function of the time lag between them. The analysis of _____ is a mathematical tool for finding repeating patterns, such as the presence of a periodic signal obscured by noise, or identifying the missing fundamental frequency in a signal implied by its harmonic frequencies. It is often used in signal processing for analyzing functions or series of values, such as time domain signals.

Exam Probability: **Medium**

35. *Answer choices:*

(see index for correct answer)

- a. Compressed sensing
- b. Smearing retransformation
- c. Semiparametric regression
- d. Autocorrelation

Guidance: level 1

:: Time series analysis ::

The _____ test is a statistical hypothesis test for determining whether one time series is useful in forecasting another, first proposed in 1969. Ordinarily, regressions reflect "mere" correlations, but Clive Granger argued that causality in economics could be tested for by measuring the ability to predict the future values of a time series using prior values of another time series. Since the question of "true causality" is deeply philosophical, and because of the post hoc ergo propter hoc fallacy of assuming that one thing preceding another can be used as a proof of causation, econometricians assert that the Granger test finds only "predictive causality".

Exam Probability: **Medium**

36. *Answer choices:*

(see index for correct answer)

- a. Spike-triggered covariance
- b. Lulu smoothing
- c. Granger causality
- d. Threshold model

Guidance: level 1

:: Seasonality ::

In time series data, _____ is the presence of variations that occur at specific regular intervals less than a year, such as weekly, monthly, or quarterly. _____ may be caused by various factors, such as weather, vacation, and holidays and consists of periodic, repetitive, and generally regular and predictable patterns in the levels of a time series.

37. *Answer choices:*

(see index for correct answer)

- a. Seasonality
- b. Seasonally adjusted annual rate
- c. Seasonal effects on suicide rates
- d. Season of birth

Guidance: level 1

:: Underlying principles of microeconomic behavior ::

The _____ is a result about the differentiability properties of the objective function of a parameterized optimization problem. As we change parameters of the objective, the _____ shows that, in a certain sense, changes in the optimizer of the objective do not contribute to the change in the objective function. The _____ is an important tool for comparative statics of optimization models.

Exam Probability: **Low**

38. *Answer choices:*

(see index for correct answer)

- a. Agent
- b. Envelope theorem

- c. Self-interest
- d. Homo reciprocans

Guidance: level 1

:: Data collection ::

A _____ is an utterance which typically functions as a request for information. _____ s can thus be understood as a kind of illocutionary act in the field of pragmatics or as special kinds of propositions in frameworks of formal semantics such as alternative semantics or inquisitive semantics. The information requested is expected to be provided in the form of an answer. _____ s are often conflated with interrogatives, which are the grammatical forms typically used to achieve them. Rhetorical _____ s, for example, are interrogative in form but may not be considered true _____ s as they are not expected to be answered. Conversely, non-interrogative grammatical structures may be considered _____ s as in the case of the imperative sentence "tell me your name".

Exam Probability: **Medium**

39. *Answer choices:*

(see index for correct answer)

- a. Question
- b. Datalogix
- c. Data farming
- d. Computer-assisted telephone interviewing

:: Statistical charts and diagrams ::

A _____ is a diagram that shows all possible logical relations between a finite collection of different sets. These diagrams depict elements as points in the plane, and sets as regions inside closed curves. A _____ consists of multiple overlapping closed curves, usually circles, each representing a set. The points inside a curve labelled S represent elements of the set S, while points outside the boundary represent elements not in the set S. This lends to easily read visualizations; for example, the set of all elements that are members of both sets S and T, S n T, is represented visually by the area of overlap of the regions S and T. In _____ s the curves are overlapped in every possible way, showing all possible relations between the sets. They are thus a special case of Euler diagrams, which do not necessarily show all relations. _____ s were conceived around 1880 by John Venn. They are used to teach elementary set theory, as well as illustrate simple set relationships in probability, logic, statistics, linguistics, and computer science.

Exam Probability: **High**

40. *Answer choices:*

(see index for correct answer)

- a. CUSUM
- b. Venn diagram
- c. Pie chart
- d. Dendrogram

:: Causal inference ::

_____ is the extent to which a piece of evidence supports a claim about cause and effect, within the context of a particular study. It is one of the most important properties of scientific studies, and is an important concept in reasoning about evidence more generally. _____ is determined by how well a study can rule out alternative explanations for its findings . It contrasts with external validity, the extent to which results can justify conclusions about other contexts .

Exam Probability: **High**

41. *Answer choices:*

(see index for correct answer)

- a. External validity
- b. Probabilistic causation
- c. Qualitative comparative analysis
- d. Internal validity

:: Statistical charts and diagrams ::

A _____ , named after Vilfredo Pareto, is a type of chart that contains both bars and a line graph, where individual values are represented in descending order by bars, and the cumulative total is represented by the line.

Exam Probability: **Medium**

42. *Answer choices:*

(see index for correct answer)

- a. EWMA chart
- b. Probability plot
- c. Dot plot
- d. Pareto chart

Guidance: level 1

:: Statistical inference ::

A _____ is a statistical interval within which, with some confidence level, a specified proportion of a sampled population falls. "More specifically, a 100×p%/100× _____ provides limits within which at least a certain proportion of the population falls with a given level of confidence ."
"A _____ based on a sample is constructed so that it would include at least a proportion p of the sampled population with confidence 1-a; such a TI is usually referred to as p-content - coverage TI." "A upper tolerance limit is simply a 1-a upper confidence limit for the 100 p percentile of the population."

43. *Answer choices:*

(see index for correct answer)

- a. Pseudolikelihood
- b. Well-behaved statistic
- c. Support curve
- d. Null distribution

Guidance: level 1

:: Regression analysis ::

In statistics, the _____ model , is an ordinal regression model—that is, a regression model for ordinal dependent variables—first considered by Peter McCullagh. For example, if one question on a survey is to be answered by a choice among "poor", "fair", "good", and "excellent", and the purpose of the analysis is to see how well that response can be predicted by the responses to other questions, some of which may be quantitative, then ordered logistic regression may be used. It can be thought of as an extension of the logistic regression model that applies to dichotomous dependent variables, allowing for more than two response categories.

44. *Answer choices:*

(see index for correct answer)

- a. Multinomial probit
- b. Proportional hazards model
- c. Ordered logit
- d. Canonical analysis

Guidance: level 1

:: Statistical tests ::

A _____ is any statistical test for which the distribution of the test statistic under the null hypothesis can be approximated by a normal distribution. Because of the central limit theorem, many test statistics are approximately normally distributed for large samples. For each significance level, the _____ has a single critical value which makes it more convenient than the Student`s t-test which has separate critical values for each sample size. Therefore, many statistical tests can be conveniently performed as approximate _____ s if the sample size is large or the population variance is known. If the population variance is unknown and the sample size is not large , the Student`s t-test may be more appropriate.

Exam Probability: **Medium**

45. *Answer choices:*

(see index for correct answer)

- a. ABX test
- b. Separation test
- c. False positive rate
- d. Z-test

:: Econometrics ::

In statistics, a _____ is a statistical model based on a zero-inflated probability distribution, i.e. a distribution that allows for frequent zero-valued observations.

Exam Probability: **High**

46. *Answer choices:*

(see index for correct answer)

- a. Economic statistics
- b. Unit root
- c. Zero-inflated model
- d. Epps effect

:: Mathematical economics ::

A _____ is commonly referred to as a monetary value assigned to currently unknowable or difficult-to-calculate costs. It is based on the willingness to pay principle - in the absence of market prices, the most accurate measure of the value of a good or service is what people are willing to give up in order to get it. Shadow pricing is often calculated on certain assumptions and premises. As a result, it is subjective and somewhat imprecise and inaccurate. The origin of these costs is typically due to an externalization of costs or an unwillingness to recalculate a system to account for marginal production. For example, consider a firm that already has a factory full of equipment and staff. They might estimate the _____ for a few more units of production as simply the cost of the overtime. In this manner, some goods and services have near zero _____ s, for example information goods. Less formally, a _____ can be thought of as the cost of decisions made at the margin without consideration for the total cost.

Exam Probability: **High**

47. *Answer choices:*

(see index for correct answer)

- a. Maximum theorem
- b. Shadow price
- c. Transportation theory
- d. DNSS point

Guidance: level 1

:: Consumer theory ::

In microeconomics, a consumer's _____ correspondence is the demand of a consumer over a bundle of goods that minimizes their expenditure while delivering a fixed level of utility. If the correspondence is actually a function, it is referred to as the _____ function, or compensated demand function. The function is named after John Hicks.

Exam Probability: **Medium**

48. *Answer choices:*

(see index for correct answer)

- a. Hicksian demand function
- b. Marginal rate of substitution
- c. Demand vacuum
- d. Hicksian demand

Guidance: level 1

:: Fundamental analysis ::

_____ s are narrowly interconnected with the concepts of value, interest rate and liquidity.A _____ that shall happen on a future day tN can be transformed into a _____ of the same value in t0.

Exam Probability: **Low**

49. *Answer choices:*

(see index for correct answer)

- a. Restricted stock
- b. First Chicago Method
- c. Net income per employee
- d. Cash flow

Guidance: level 1

:: Seasonality ::

_____ is a statistical method for removing the seasonal component of a time series that exhibits a seasonal pattern. It is usually done when wanting to analyse the trend, and cyclical deviations from trend, of a time series independently of the seasonal components. It is normal to report seasonally adjusted data for unemployment rates to reveal the underlying trends and cycles in labor markets. Many economic phenomena have seasonal cycles, such as agricultural production and consumer consumption, e.g. greater consumption leading up to Christmas. It is necessary to adjust for this component in order to understand what underlying trends are in the economy and so official statistics are often adjusted to remove seasonal components.

Exam Probability: **Low**

50. *Answer choices:*

(see index for correct answer)

- a. Season of birth
- b. Seasonal adjustment

- c. Seasonal effects on suicide rates
- d. Seasonality

Guidance: level 1

:: Statistical inference ::

In statistical hypothesis testing,the _____ and the null hypothesis are the two rival hypotheses which are compared by a statistical hypothesis test.

Exam Probability: **Low**

51. *Answer choices:*

(see index for correct answer)

- a. Quasi-likelihood
- b. Consistent estimator
- c. Confidence distribution
- d. Uncomfortable science

Guidance: level 1

:: Goods ::

In economics and consumer theory, a _____ is a product that people consume more of as the price rises and vice versa—violating the basic law of demand in microeconomics. For any other sort of good, as the price of the good rises, the substitution effect makes consumers purchase less of it, and more of substitute goods; for most goods, the income effect reinforces this decline in demand for the good. But a _____ is so strongly an inferior good in the minds of consumers that this contrary income effect more than offsets the substitution effect, and the net effect of the good's price rise is to increase demand for it.

Exam Probability: **High**

52. *Answer choices:*

(see index for correct answer)

- a. excludable
- b. Yellow goods
- c. Public good
- d. Free good

Guidance: level 1

:: Income ::

_____ is the consumption and saving opportunity gained by an entity within a specified timeframe, which is generally expressed in monetary terms. For households and individuals, " _____ is the sum of all the wages, salaries, profits, interest payments, rents, and other forms of earnings received in a given period of time."

53. *Answer choices:*

(see index for correct answer)

- a. Income
- b. Per capita income
- c. Total personal income
- d. Signing bonus

Guidance: level 1

:: Regression analysis ::

In statistics, the _____ , alternatively known as the model sum of squares or sum of squares due to regression , is a quantity used in describing how well a model, often a regression model, represents the data being modelled. In particular, the _____ measures how much variation there is in the modelled values and this is compared to the total sum of squares, which measures how much variation there is in the observed data, and to the residual sum of squares, which measures the variation in the modelling errors.

54. *Answer choices:*

(see index for correct answer)

- a. Mixed model

- b. Deming regression
- c. Polynomial regression
- d. Explained sum of squares

Guidance: level 1

:: Statistical terminology ::

In mathematical modeling, statistical modeling and experimental sciences, the values of _____ s depend on the values of in _____ s. The _____ s represent the output or outcome whose variation is being studied. The in _____ s, also known in a statistical context as regressors, represent inputs or causes, that is, potential reasons for variation. In an experiment, any variable that the experimenter manipulates can be called an in _____ . Models and experiments test the effects that the in _____ s have on the _____ s. Sometimes, even if their influence is not of direct interest, in _____ s may be included for other reasons, such as to account for their potential confounding effect.

Exam Probability: **Medium**

55. *Answer choices:*
(see index for correct answer)

- a. Core damage frequency
- b. Noncentrality parameter
- c. Shape parameter
- d. Strong prior

:: Combinatorial game theory ::

A _____ is an astronomical object consisting of a luminous spheroid of plasma held together by its own gravity. The nearest _____ to Earth is the Sun. Many other _____ s are visible to the naked eye from Earth during the night, appearing as a multitude of fixed luminous points in the sky due to their immense distance from Earth. Historically, the most prominent _____ s were grouped into constellations and asterisms, the brightest of which gained proper names. Astronomers have assembled _____ catalogues that identify the known _____ s and provide standardized stellar designations. However, most of the estimated 300 sextillion _____ s in the Universe are invisible to the naked eye from Earth, including all _____ s outside our galaxy, the Milky Way.

Exam Probability: **Low**

56. *Answer choices:*

(see index for correct answer)

- a. Map-coloring games
- b. Impartial game
- c. Star
- d. Indistinguishability quotient

:: Mathematical and quantitative methods (economics) ::

In mathematics, a _____ is a result saying that a function F will have at least one fixed point , under some conditions on F that can be stated in general terms. Results of this kind are amongst the most generally useful in mathematics.

Exam Probability: **Medium**

57. *Answer choices:*

(see index for correct answer)

- a. Heteroscedasticity-consistent standard errors
- b. Multinomial logistic regression
- c. Fixed-point theorem
- d. Oxford model

Guidance: level 1

:: Statistical forecasting ::

A _____ occurs when there are consistent differences between actual outcomes and previously generated forecasts of those quantities; that is: forecasts may have a general tendency to be too high or too low. A normal property of a good forecast is that it is not biased.

Exam Probability: **Low**

(see index for correct answer)

- a. Demand forecasting
- b. Calculating demand forecast accuracy
- c. Meteorological reanalysis
- d. Data assimilation

Guidance: level 1

:: Regression analysis ::

In statistics, _____ is a technique for estimating the unknown parameters in a linear regression model when there is a certain degree of correlation between the residuals in a regression model. In these cases, ordinary least squares and weighted least squares can be statistically inefficient, or even give misleading inferences. GLS was first described by Alexander Aitken in 1934.

Exam Probability: **Medium**

59. *Answer choices:*

(see index for correct answer)

- a. Generalized least squares
- b. Moderation
- c. Bayesian linear regression
- d. Antecedent variable

Guidance: level 1

Microeconomics

Microeconomics analyzes basic elements in the economy, including individual agents and markets, their interactions, and the outcomes of interactions. Individual agents may include, for example, households, firms, buyers, and sellers.

:: Economics terminology ::

In economics, an externality is the cost or benefit that affects a party who did not choose to incur that cost or benefit. Externalities often occur when a product or service's price equilibrium cannot reflect the true costs and benefits of that product or service. This causes the externality competitive equilibrium to not be a Pareto optimality.

Exam Probability: **High**

1. *Answer choices:*

(see index for correct answer)

- a. External cost
- b. Profit motive
- c. Substantivism
- d. Base period

Guidance: level 1

:: Microeconomics ::

In financial accounting, an _____ is any resource owned by the business. Anything tangible or intangible that can be owned or controlled to produce value and that is held by a company to produce positive economic value is an _____ . Simply stated, _____ s represent value of ownership that can be converted into cash . The balance sheet of a firm records the monetary value of the _____ s owned by that firm. It covers money and other valuables belonging to an individual or to a business.

2. *Answer choices:*

(see index for correct answer)

- a. Marginal factor cost
- b. Asset
- c. Consumer sovereignty
- d. Local nonsatiation

Guidance: level 1

:: Consumer theory ::

In economics, the _____ is the rate at which a consumer can give up some amount of one good in exchange for another good while maintaining the same level of utility. At equilibrium consumption levels , marginal rates of substitution are identical. The _____ is one of the three factors from marginal productivity, the others being marginal rates of transformation and marginal productivity of a factor.

Exam Probability: **Medium**

3. *Answer choices:*

(see index for correct answer)

- a. Snob effect
- b. Permanent income hypothesis

- c. Marginal rate of substitution
- d. Marshallian demand

Guidance: level 1

:: Socioeconomics ::

_____ is the amount of goods and services that can be purchased with a unit of currency. For example, if one had taken one unit of currency to a store in the 1950s, it would have been possible to buy a greater number of items than would be the case today, indicating that the currency had a greater _____ in the 1950s. Currency can be either a commodity money, like gold or silver, or fiat money emitted by government sanctioned agencies.

Exam Probability: **Medium**

4. *Answer choices:*
(see index for correct answer)

- a. Employability
- b. Purchasing power
- c. Transcendental homelessness
- d. Sabbath economics

Guidance: level 1

:: Capitalist systems ::

_____ is an economic system based on the private ownership of the means of production and their operation for profit. Characteristics central to _____ include private property, capital accumulation, wage labor, voluntary exchange, a price system, and competitive markets. In a capitalist market economy, decision-making and investment are determined by every owner of wealth, property or production ability in financial and capital markets, whereas prices and the distribution of goods and services are mainly determined by competition in goods and services markets.

Exam Probability: **Medium**

5. *Answer choices:*

(see index for correct answer)

- a. New economy
- b. Capitalism
- c. Technocapitalism
- d. Coordinated market economy

Guidance: level 1

:: Price controls ::

_____ are governmental restrictions on the prices that can be charged for goods and services in a market. The intent behind implementing such controls can stem from the desire to maintain affordability of goods even during shortages, and to slow inflation, or, alternatively, to ensure a minimum income for providers of certain goods or a minimum wage. There are two primary forms of price control, a price ceiling, the maximum price that can be charged, and a price floor, the minimum price that can be charged.

Exam Probability: **Medium**

6. *Answer choices:*

(see index for correct answer)

- a. Price controls
- b. Price support
- c. Edict on Maximum Prices
- d. Actual GDP

Guidance: level 1

:: Markets (customer bases) ::

In economics, the theory of _____ s, associated primarily with its 1982 proponent William J. Baumol, holds that there are markets served by a small number of firms that are nevertheless characterized by competitive equilibria because of the existence of potential short-term entrants.

Exam Probability: **Medium**

7. *Answer choices:*

(see index for correct answer)

- a. Economic equilibrium
- b. Competitive equilibrium
- c. Contestable market
- d. Vertical market

Guidance: level 1

:: Rationing and licensing ::

_____ is the controlled distribution of scarce resources, goods, services, or an artificial restriction of demand. _____ controls the size of the ration, which is one's allowed portion of the resources being distributed on a particular day or at a particular time. There are many forms of _____ , and in western civilization people experience some of them in daily life without realizing it.

Exam Probability: **High**

8. *Answer choices:*

(see index for correct answer)

- a. Schweinemord
- b. Utility furniture
- c. Meat-free day
- d. Bratt System

:: Socioeconomics ::

_____ is the right to exercise power, which can be formalized by a state and exercised by way of judges, appointed executives of government, or the ecclesiastical or priestly appointed representatives of a God or other deities.

Exam Probability: **High**

9. *Answer choices:*

(see index for correct answer)

- a. Economic sociology
- b. Social mobility
- c. Authority
- d. Transcendental homelessness

:: Microeconomics ::

In economics, an _____ or economic surplus is a situation in which the quantity of a good or service supplied is more than the quantity demanded, and the price is above the equilibrium level determined by supply and demand. That is, the quantity of the product that producers wish to sell exceeds the quantity that potential buyers are willing to buy at the prevailing price. It is the opposite of an economic shortage .

Exam Probability: **Low**

10. *Answer choices:*

(see index for correct answer)

- a. Excess supply
- b. Forced rider
- c. Ex-ante
- d. Total cost

Guidance: level 1

:: Microeconomics ::

In economics, a _____ gives the technological relation between quantities of physical inputs and quantities of output of goods. The _____ is one of the key concepts of mainstream neoclassical theories, used to define marginal product and to distinguish allocative efficiency, a key focus of economics. One important purpose of the _____ is to address allocative efficiency in the use of factor inputs in production and the resulting distribution of income to those factors, while abstracting away from the technological problems of achieving technical efficiency, as an engineer or professional manager might understand it.

Exam Probability: **Medium**

11. *Answer choices:*

(see index for correct answer)

- a. Production function
- b. RevPAR
- c. Search cost
- d. Economies of scope

Guidance: level 1

:: Utilitarianism ::

_____ is a family of consequentialist ethical theories that promotes actions that maximize happiness and well-being for the majority of a population. Although different varieties of _____ admit different characterizations, the basic idea behind all of them is to in some sense maximize utility, which is often defined in terms of well-being or related concepts. For instance, Jeremy Bentham, the founder of _____ , described utility as

Exam Probability: **Medium**

12. *Answer choices:*

(see index for correct answer)

- • a. Utilitarianism
- • b. Utility monster
- • c. Preference utilitarianism
- • d. Paradox of hedonism

Guidance: level 1

:: Capital (economics) ::

_____ is any economic resource measured in terms of money used by entrepreneurs and businesses to buy what they need to make their products or to provide their services to the sector of the economy upon which their operation is based, i.e. retail, corporate, investment banking, etc.

Exam Probability: **High**

13. *Answer choices:*

(see index for correct answer)

- a. Financial capital
- b. Instructional capital
- c. Information capital
- d. Dead capital

Guidance: level 1

:: Production economics ::

An _____ is a contour line drawn through the set of points at which the same quantity of output is produced while changing the quantities of two or more inputs. While an indifference curve mapping helps to solve the utility-maximizing problem of consumers, the _____ mapping deals with the cost-minimization problem of producers. _____ s are typically drawn along with isocost curves in capital-labor graphs, showing the technological tradeoff between capital and labor in the production function, and the decreasing marginal returns of both inputs. Adding one input while holding the other constant eventually leads to decreasing marginal output, and this is reflected in the shape of the _____ . A family of _____ s can be represented by an _____ map, a graph combining a number of _____ s, each representing a different quantity of output. _____ s are also called equal product curves.

Exam Probability: **Low**

14. *Answer choices:*

(see index for correct answer)

- a. Split-off point
- b. Capacity utilization
- c. Factor price
- d. Marginal product of labor

Guidance: level 1

:: Scarcity ::

_____ is the limited availability of a commodity, which may be in demand in the market. _____ also includes an individual's lack of resources to buy commodities.

Exam Probability: **Low**

15. *Answer choices:*

(see index for correct answer)

- a. Scarcity
- b. Economic rent
- c. Deadweight loss
- d. Thoughts and Details on Scarcity

Guidance: level 1

:: Demand ::

_____ is the quantity of a good that consumers are willing and able to purchase at various prices during a given period of time.

Exam Probability: **Medium**

16. *Answer choices:*

(see index for correct answer)

- a. Marginal demand
- b. Demand sensing
- c. Effective demand
- d. Demand

Guidance: level 1

:: Trade union legislation ::

The National Labor Relations Act of 1935 is a foundational statute of United States labor law which guarantees the right of private sector employees to organize into trade unions, engage in collective bargaining, and take collective action such as strikes. The act was written by Senator Robert F. Wagner, passed by the 74th United States Congress, and signed into law by President Franklin D. Roosevelt.

Exam Probability: **Medium**

17. *Answer choices:*

(see index for correct answer)

- a. Employment Act 1982
- b. Padlock Law
- c. Wagner Act
- d. National Labor Relations Act

Guidance: level 1

:: Microeconomics ::

_____ are "efficiencies formed by variety, not volume". For example, a gas station that sells gasoline can sell soda, milk, baked goods, etc through their customer service representatives and thus achieve gasoline companies _____ .

Exam Probability: **Low**

18. *Answer choices:*
(see index for correct answer)

- a. Revenue Technology Services
- b. Relative price
- c. Economies of scope
- d. Product proliferation

Guidance: level 1

:: Competition law ::

Competition law is a law that promotes or seeks to maintain market competition by regulating anti-competitive conduct by companies. Competition law is implemented through public and private enforcement. Competition law is known as " _____ " in the United States for historical reasons, and as "anti-monopoly law" in China and Russia. In previous years it has been known as trade practices law in the United Kingdom and Australia. In the European Union, it is referred to as both antitrust and competition law.

Exam Probability: **Medium**

19. *Answer choices:*
(see index for correct answer)

- a. Illegal per se
- b. Vertical agreement
- c. Caselex
- d. Antitrust law

Guidance: level 1

:: Microeconomics ::

A reservation price is a limit on the price of a good or a service. On the demand side, it is the highest price that a buyer is willing to pay; on the supply side, it is the lowest price at which a seller is willing to sell a good or service. _____ s are commonly used in auctions, but the concept is extended beyond.

Exam Probability: **Low**

20. *Answer choices:*

(see index for correct answer)

- a. Reservation price
- b. Production set
- c. Missing market
- d. Lexicographic preferences

Guidance: level 1

:: Types of business entity ::

A _____ , also known as the sole trader, individual entrepreneurship or proprietorship, is a type of enterprise that is owned and run by one person and in which there is no legal distinction between the owner and the business entity. A sole trader does not necessarily work `alone`—it is possible for the sole trader to employ other people.

Exam Probability: **High**

21. *Answer choices:*

(see index for correct answer)

- a. privately held
- b. Sole proprietorship

Guidance: level 1

:: Taxation ::

A _____ is a tax incentive which allows certain taxpayers to subtract the amount of the credit they have accrued from the total they owe the state. It may also be a credit granted in recognition of taxes already paid or, as in the United Kingdom, a form of state support.

Exam Probability: **Medium**

22. *Answer choices:*

(see index for correct answer)

- a. Tax credit
- b. Fiscal burden of government
- c. Fin 48
- d. Energy tax

Guidance: level 1

:: Entrepreneurship ::

_____ is the process of designing, launching and running a new business, which is often initially a small business. The people who create these businesses are called entrepreneurs.

Exam Probability: **Medium**

23. *Answer choices:*

(see index for correct answer)

- a. Mompreneur
- b. Inclusive entrepreneurship
- c. Stealth startup
- d. Community business development corporation

Guidance: level 1

:: Economics terminology ::

In economics, _____ or just capital is a factor of production , consisting of machinery, buildings, computers, and the like. The production function takes the general form Y=f, where Y is the amount of output produced, K is the amount of capital stock used, L is the amount of labor used, and N is the amount of natural resources used. In economic theory, _____ is one of the three primary factors of production; the others are natural resources , and laborthe stock of competences embodied in the labor force. _____ is distinct from human capital , circulating capital, and financial capital. _____ is fixed capital, which is any kind of real physical asset that is not used up in the production of a product. Usually the value of land is not included in _____ as it is not a reproducible product of human activities.

Exam Probability: **Low**

24. *Answer choices:*

(see index for correct answer)

- a. Head count ratio
- b. Decoupling plus
- c. Electronic payment advice
- d. Economic unit

Guidance: level 1

:: Business economics ::

In economics, _____ is demand for a factor of production or intermediate good that occurs as a result of the demand for another intermediate or final good. In essence, the demand for, say, a factor of production by a firm is dependent on the demand by consumers for the product produced by the firm. The term was first introduced by Alfred Marshall in his Principles of Economics in 1890.

Exam Probability: **Low**

25. *Answer choices:*

(see index for correct answer)

- a. Derived demand
- b. Pricing science
- c. shareholders
- d. Vendor finance

Guidance: level 1

:: Patent law ::

A _____ is a form of intellectual property that gives its owner the legal right to exclude others from making, using, selling, and importing an invention for a limited period of years, in exchange for publishing an enabling public disclosure of the invention. In most countries _____ rights fall under civil law and the _____ holder needs to sue someone infringing the _____ in order to enforce his or her rights. In some industries _____ s are an essential form of competitive advantage; in others they are irrelevant.

26. *Answer choices:*

(see index for correct answer)

- a. Technological alliance
- b. Free license
- c. Patentleft
- d. Patent

Guidance: level 1

:: Progressive Era in the United States ::

The Sherman Antitrust Act of 1890 was a United States antitrust law that regulates competition among enterprises, which was passed by Congress under the presidency of Benjamin Harrison.

Exam Probability: **Medium**

27. *Answer choices:*

(see index for correct answer)

- a. Sherman Antitrust Act
- b. Sherman Act

Guidance: level 1

:: Social security ::

Unemployment benefits are payments made by back authorized bodies to unemployed people. In the United States, benefits are funded by a compulsory governmental insurance system, not taxes on individual citizens. Depending on the jurisdiction and the status of the person, those sums may be small, covering only basic needs, or may compensate the lost time proportionally to the previous earned salary.

Exam Probability: **Medium**

28. *Answer choices:*

(see index for correct answer)

- a. Unemployment compensation
- b. Social Security System
- c. Social security in Sweden
- d. Employees%27 State Insurance

Guidance: level 1

:: Costs ::

_____ in neoclassical economics is the sum of the private costs resulting from a transaction and the costs imposed on the consumers as a consequence of being exposed to the transaction for which they are not compensated or charged. In other words it is the sum of personal and external costs. Private costs refer to direct costs to the producer for producing the good or service. _____ includes these private costs and the additional costs associated with the production of the good for which are not accounted for by the free market. Mathematically, social marginal cost is the sum of private marginal cost and the external costs. For example, when selling a glass of lemonade at a lemonade stand, the private costs involved in this transaction are the costs of the lemons and the sugar and the water that are ingredients to the lemonade, the opportunity cost of the labor to combine them into lemonade, as well as any transaction costs, such as walking to the stand. An example of marginal damages associated with _____ s of driving includes wear and tear, congestion, and the decreased quality of life due to drunks driving or impatience.a large number of people displaced from their homes and localities due to construction work.

Exam Probability: **Low**

29. *Answer choices:*

(see index for correct answer)

- a. Explicit cost
- b. Social cost
- c. Variable Costing
- d. Psychic cost

Guidance: level 1

:: Transport economics ::

_____ or congestion charges is a system of surcharging users of public goods that are subject to congestion through excess demand such as higher peak charges for use of bus services, electricity, metros, railways, telephones, and road pricing to reduce traffic congestion; airlines and shipping companies may be charged higher fees for slots at airports and through canals at busy times. Advocates claim this pricing strategy regulates demand, making it possible to manage congestion without increasing supply.

Exam Probability: **Low**

30. *Answer choices:*

(see index for correct answer)

- a. Caphar
- b. Congestion pricing
- c. Vignette
- d. Space elevator economics

Guidance: level 1

:: Monopoly (economics) ::

A _____ exists when a specific person or enterprise is the only supplier of a particular commodity. This contrasts with a monopsony which relates to a single entity's control of a market to purchase a good or service, and with oligopoly which consists of a few sellers dominating a market. Monopolies are thus characterized by a lack of economic competition to produce the good or service, a lack of viable substitute goods, and the possibility of a high _____ price well above the seller's marginal cost that leads to a high _____ profit. The verb monopolise or monopolize refers to the process by which a company gains the ability to raise prices or exclude competitors. In economics, a _____ is a single seller. In law, a _____ is a business entity that has significant market power, that is, the power to charge overly high prices. Although monopolies may be big businesses, size is not a characteristic of a _____ . A small business may still have the power to raise prices in a small industry .

Exam Probability: **Low**

31. *Answer choices:*

(see index for correct answer)

- a. Practice of law
- b. Legal monopoly
- c. Monopoly
- d. Tesco Town

Guidance: level 1

:: Economics curves ::

In economics, the _____ is a graphical representation of the distribution of income or of wealth. It was developed by Max O. Lorenz in 1905 for representing inequality of the wealth distribution.

Exam Probability: **Medium**

32. *Answer choices:*

(see index for correct answer)

- a. Cost curve
- b. Hubbert curve
- c. Lorenz curve
- d. Marginal propensity to save

Guidance: level 1

:: Tax incidence ::

In economics, _____ or tax burden is the effect of a particular tax on the distribution of economic welfare. Economists distinguish between the entities who ultimately bear the tax burden and those on whom tax is initially imposed. The tax burden measures the true economic weight of the tax, measured by the difference between real incomes or utilities before and after imposing the tax. An individuality on whom the tax is levied does not have to bear the true size of the tax. For the example of this difference, assume a firm, that contains employer and employees. The tax imposed on the employer is divided. The concept of _____ was initially brought to economists' attention by the French Physiocrats, in particular François Quesnay, who argued that the incidence of all taxation falls ultimately on landowners and is at the expense of land rent. _____ is said to "fall" upon the group that ultimately bears the burden of, or ultimately suffers a loss from, the tax. The key concept of _____ is that the _____ or tax burden does not depend on where the revenue is collected, but on the price elasticity of demand and price elasticity of supply. As a general policy matter, the _____ should not violate the principles of a desirable tax system, especially fairness and transparency.

Exam Probability: **Low**

33. *Answer choices:*

(see index for correct answer)

- a. tax burden
- b. Stealth tax
- c. Tax incidence
- d. excess burden of taxation

Guidance: level 1

:: Asymmetric information ::

_____ is a term commonly used in economics, insurance, and risk management that describes a situation where market participation is affected by asymmetric information. When buyers and sellers have different information, it is known as a state of asymmetric information. Traders with better private information about the quality of a product will selectively participate in trades which benefit them the most, at the expense of the other trader. A textbook example is Akerlof's market for lemons.

Exam Probability: **High**

34. *Answer choices:*

(see index for correct answer)

- a. Single-crossing
- b. Pooling equilibrium
- c. Adverse selection
- d. Agency cost

Guidance: level 1

:: Progressive Era in the United States ::

The _____ of 1890 was a United States antitrust law that regulates competition among enterprises, which was passed by Congress under the presidency of Benjamin Harrison.

35. *Answer choices:*

(see index for correct answer)

- a. Sherman Act
- b. Sherman Antitrust Act

Guidance: level 1

:: Renewable resources ::

A _____ is a natural resource which will replenish to replace the portion depleted by usage and consumption, either through natural reproduction or other recurring processes in a finite amount of time in a human time scale. _____ s are a part of Earth's natural environment and the largest components of its ecosphere. A positive life cycle assessment is a key indicator of a resource's sustainability.

36. *Answer choices:*

(see index for correct answer)

- a. Proteak
- b. Consortium for Research on Renewable Industrial Materials
- c. Renewable resource
- d. renewable

:: History of banking ::

A _____ is a monetary system in which the standard economic unit of account is based on a fixed quantity of gold. Three types can be distinguished: specie, bullion, and exchange.

Exam Probability: **Medium**

37. *Answer choices:*

(see index for correct answer)

- a. Henry Hope
- b. Gold standard
- c. Fould family
- d. Rothschild family

:: Costs ::

In economics, _____ s, indirect costs or overheads are business expenses that are not dependent on the level of goods or services produced by the business. They tend to be time-related, such as interest or rents being paid per month, and are often referred to as overhead costs. This is in contrast to variable costs, which are volume-related and unknown at the beginning of the accounting year. For a simple example, such as a bakery, the monthly rent for the baking facilities, and the monthly payments for the security system and basic phone line are _____ s, as they do not change according to how much bread the bakery produces and sells. On the other hand, the wage costs of the bakery are variable, as the bakery will have to hire more workers if the production of bread increases. Economists reckon _____ as a entry barrier for new entrepreneurs.

Exam Probability: **Medium**

38. *Answer choices:*

(see index for correct answer)

- a. Fixed cost
- b. Social cost
- c. Cost driver
- d. Cost of products sold

Guidance: level 1

:: Economics terminology ::

_____ is the total receipts a seller can obtain from selling goods or services to buyers. It can be written as P × Q, which is the price of the goods multiplied by the quantity of the sold goods.

Exam Probability: **High**

39. *Answer choices:*

(see index for correct answer)

- a. money creation
- b. Sampo generation
- c. Effectiveness
- d. Capital good

Guidance: level 1

:: Cartels ::

A _____ is a group of apparently independent producers whose goal is to increase their collective profits by means of price fixing, limiting supply, or other restrictive practices. _____ s typically control selling prices, but some are organized to control the prices of purchased inputs. Antitrust laws attempt to deter or forbid _____ s. A single entity that holds a monopoly by this definition cannot be a _____ , though it may be guilty of abusing said monopoly in other ways. _____ s usually occur in oligopolies, where there are a small number of sellers and usually involve homogeneous products.

Exam Probability: **High**

40. *Answer choices:*

(see index for correct answer)

- a. Canpotex
- b. Cartel
- c. Copper cartels
- d. Organization of Petroleum Importing Countries

Guidance: level 1

:: Game theory ::

In game theory, the _____ , named after the mathematician John Forbes Nash Jr., is a proposed solution of a non-cooperative game involving two or more players in which each player is assumed to know the equilibrium strategies of the other players, and no player has anything to gain by changing only their own strategy.

Exam Probability: **Low**

41. *Answer choices:*

(see index for correct answer)

- a. Bulk Dispatch Lapse
- b. Pursuit-evasion
- c. Nash equilibrium
- d. Subgame perfect equilibrium

:: Scarcity ::

In economics, _____ is any payment to an owner or factor of production in excess of the costs needed to bring that factor into production. In classical economics, _____ is any payment made or benefit received for non-produced inputs such as location and for assets formed by creating official privilege over natural opportunities . In the moral economy of neoclassical economics, _____ includes income gained by labor or state beneficiaries of other "contrived" exclusivity, such as labor guilds and unofficial corruption.

Exam Probability: **High**

42. *Answer choices:*

(see index for correct answer)

- a. Post-Scarcity Anarchism
- b. Artificial scarcity
- c. Economic rent
- d. Deadweight loss

:: Financial markets ::

In economics, _____ is the process by which, in an economic market, the supply of whatever is traded is equated to the demand, so that there is no leftover supply or demand. The new classical economics assumes that, in any given market, assuming that all buyers and sellers have access to information and that there is not "friction" impeding price changes, prices always adjust up or down to ensure _____ .

Exam Probability: **High**

43. *Answer choices:*

(see index for correct answer)

- a. No free lunch with vanishing risk
- b. Exchange of futures for swaps
- c. Turquoise
- d. Security analysis

Guidance: level 1

:: Monetary economics ::

_____ is any item or verifiable record that is generally accepted as payment for goods and services and repayment of debts, such as taxes, in a particular country or socio-economic context. The main functions of _____ are distinguished as: a medium of exchange, a unit of account, a store of value and sometimes, a standard of deferred payment. Any item or verifiable record that fulfils these functions can be considered as _____ .

44. *Answer choices:*

(see index for correct answer)

- a. Money
- b. Near money
- c. Monetary circuit theory
- d. Price level

Guidance: level 1

:: Health economics ::

In an insurance policy, the _____ is the amount paidout of pocket by the policy holder before an insurance provider will pay any expenses. In general usage, the term _____ may be used to describe one of several types of clauses that are used by insurance companies as a threshold for policy payments.

Exam Probability: **Low**

45. *Answer choices:*

(see index for correct answer)

- a. Deductible
- b. Pharmacoeconomics

- c. economic evaluation
- d. Community rating

Guidance: level 1

:: Economics ::

In economics, an _____ is a curve in a graph with quantities of two inputs, typically physical capital and labor, plotted on the axes. The path connects optimal input combinations as the scale of production expands. A producer seeking to produce a given number of units of a product in the cheapest possible way chooses the point on the _____ that is also on the isoquant associated with that output level.

Exam Probability: **High**

46. *Answer choices:*
(see index for correct answer)

- a. Financial compensation
- b. Jacob Marschak Lecture
- c. Expansion path
- d. Kaleidics

Guidance: level 1

:: Microeconomics ::

In mainstream economics, _____ , also known as total welfare or Marshallian surplus , refers to two related quantities. Consumer surplus or consumers' surplus is the monetary gain obtained by consumers because they are able to purchase a product for a price that is less than the highest price that they would be willing to pay. Producer surplus or producers' surplus is the amount that producers benefit by selling at a market price that is higher than the least that they would be willing to sell for; this is roughly equal to profit .

Exam Probability: **Low**

47. *Answer choices:*

(see index for correct answer)

- a. Robinson Crusoe economy
- b. Feasibility condition
- c. Market demand schedule
- d. Economic surplus

Guidance: level 1

:: Costs ::

_____ s are costs that change as the quantity of the good or service that a business produces changes. _____ s are the sum of marginal costs over all units produced. They can also be considered normal costs. Fixed costs and _____ s make up the two components of total cost. Direct costs are costs that can easily be associated with a particular cost object. However, not all _____ s are direct costs. For example, variable manufacturing overhead costs are _____ s that are indirect costs, not direct costs. _____ s are sometimes called unit-level costs as they vary with the number of units produced.

Exam Probability: **Low**

48. *Answer choices:*

(see index for correct answer)

- a. Explicit cost
- b. Variable cost
- c. Average cost
- d. Cost accounting

Guidance: level 1

:: Standard of living ::

An individual's or a socioeconomic class's _____ is the level of wealth, comfort, material goods, and necessities available to them in a certain geographic area, usually a country. The _____ includes factors such as income, quality and availability of employment, class disparity, poverty rate, quality and affordability of housing, hours of work required to purchase necessities, gross domestic product, inflation rate, amount of leisure time every year, affordable access to quality healthcare, quality and availability of education, life expectancy, incidence of disease, cost of goods and services, infrastructure, national economic growth, economic and political stability,freedom, environmental quality, climate and safety. The _____ is closely related to quality of life.

Exam Probability: **High**

49. *Answer choices:*
(see index for correct answer)

- a. Standard of living
- b. Standard of living in the United States
- c. Standard of living in Israel
- d. Standard of living in Japan

Guidance: level 1

:: United States housing bubble ::

In economics, a _____ is a business cycle contraction when there is a general decline in economic activity. Macroeconomic indicators such as GDP , investment spending, capacity utilization, household income, business profits, and inflation fall, while bankruptcies and the unemployment rate rise. In the United Kingdom, it is defined as a negative economic growth for two consecutive quarters.

Exam Probability: **Medium**

50. *Answer choices:*

(see index for correct answer)

- a. Hardest Hit Fund
- b. Predatory mortgage servicing
- c. Green shoots
- d. Recession

Guidance: level 1

:: Microeconomics ::

_____ s are a type of good in economics, sometimes classified as a subtype of public goods that are excludable but non-rivalrous, at least until reaching a point where congestion occurs. Often these goods exhibit high excludability, but at the same time low rivalry in consumption. Because of that low rivalry in consumption characteristic, _____ s have essentially zero marginal costs and are generally provided by what is commonly known as natural monopolies.Furthermore _____ s have artificial scarcity. Club theory is the area of economics that studies these goods.One of the most famous provisions was published by Buchanan in 1965 "An Economic Theory of Clubs", in which he addresses the question of how the size of the group influences the voluntary provision of a public good and more fundamentally provides a theoretical structure of communal or collective ownership-consumption arrangements.

Exam Probability: **Medium**

51. *Answer choices:*

(see index for correct answer)

- a. Revenue Technology Services
- b. RevPAR
- c. Incentive
- d. Club good

Guidance: level 1

:: Socialism ::

_____ is a range of economic and social systems characterised by social ownership of the means of production and workers' self-management, as well as the political theories and movements associated with them. Social ownership can be public, collective or cooperative ownership, or citizen ownership of equity. There are many varieties of _____ and there is no single definition encapsulating all of them, with social ownership being the common element shared by its various forms.

Exam Probability: **Medium**

52. *Answer choices:*
(see index for correct answer)

- a. Social imperialism
- b. Progg
- c. Radical Society
- d. Socialism

Guidance: level 1

:: Microeconomics ::

_____ studies the effects of psychological, cognitive, emotional, cultural and social factors on the economic decisions of individuals and institutions and how those decisions vary from those implied by classical theory.

Exam Probability: **Medium**

53. *Answer choices:*

(see index for correct answer)

- a. Yield management
- b. Inventory analysis
- c. Oligopsony
- d. Necessity good

Guidance: level 1

:: Trade policy ::

_____ is a trade policy that does not restrict imports or exports; it can also be understood as the free market idea applied to international trade. In government, _____ is predominantly advocated by political parties that hold liberal economic positions while economically left-wing and nationalist political parties generally support protectionism, the opposite of _____ .

Exam Probability: **Medium**

54. *Answer choices:*

(see index for correct answer)

- a. Green box policies
- b. Free trade
- c. Enhanced integrated framework
- d. protectionist

:: Wealth ::

_____ is the abundance of valuable financial assets or physical possessions which can be converted into a form that can be used for transactions. This includes the core meaning as held in the originating old English word weal, which is from an Indo-European word stem. A community, region or country that possesses an abundance of such possessions or resources to the benefit of the common good is known as _____ y.

Exam Probability: **Low**

55. *Answer choices:*

(see index for correct answer)

- a. Prosperity theology
- b. Captain of industry
- c. Born in the purple
- d. Wealth concentration

:: Costs ::

In economics, an _____ , also called an imputed cost, implied cost, or notional cost, is the opportunity cost equal to what a firm must give up in order to use a factor of production for which it already owns and thus does not pay rent. It is the opposite of an explicit cost, which is borne directly. In other words, an _____ is any cost that results from using an asset instead of renting it out or selling it. The term also applies to foregone income from choosing not to work.

Exam Probability: **Low**

56. *Answer choices:*

(see index for correct answer)

- a. Joint cost
- b. Cost
- c. Implicit cost
- d. Manufacturing cost

Guidance: level 1

:: Marginal concepts ::

In economics, utility is the satisfaction or benefit derived by consuming a product; thus the _____ of a good or service is the change in the utility from an increase in the consumption of that good or service.

Exam Probability: **Low**

57. *Answer choices:*

(see index for correct answer)

- a. Marginal concepts
- b. Marginal use
- c. Marginalism
- d. Marginal utility

Guidance: level 1

:: Economics ::

_____ is the social science that studies the production, distribution, and consumption of goods and services.

Exam Probability: **Medium**

58. *Answer choices:*

(see index for correct answer)

- a. Economic Club of New York
- b. Economics
- c. Internetization
- d. Manufacturing operations

Guidance: level 1

:: Project management ::

In economics, _____ is the assignment of available resources to various uses. In the context of an entire economy, resources can be allocated by various means, such as markets or central planning.

Exam Probability: **Low**

59. *Answer choices:*

(see index for correct answer)

- a. Time horizon
- b. Resource allocation

Guidance: level 1

Macroeconomics and monetary economics

Macroeconomics analyzes the entire economy (meaning aggregated production, consumption, savings, and investment) and issues affecting it, including unemployment of resources (labour, capital, and land), inflation, economic growth, and the public policies that address these issues (monetary, fiscal, and other policies).

:: Costs ::

In production, research, retail, and accounting, a _____ is the value of money that has been used up to produce something or deliver a service, and hence is not available for use anymore. In business, the _____ may be one of acquisition, in which case the amount of money expended to acquire it is counted as _____ . In this case, money is the input that is gone in order to acquire the thing. This acquisition _____ may be the sum of the _____ of production as incurred by the original producer, and further _____ s of transaction as incurred by the acquirer over and above the price paid to the producer. Usually, the price also includes a mark-up for profit over the _____ of production.

Exam Probability: **High**

1. *Answer choices:*

(see index for correct answer)

- a. Average variable cost
- b. Cost driver
- c. Implicit cost
- d. Cost

Guidance: level 1

:: Mathematical finance ::

_____ is the value of an asset at a specific date. It measures the nominal future sum of money that a given sum of money is "worth" at a specified time in the future assuming a certain interest rate, or more generally, rate of return; it is the present value multiplied by the accumulation function. The value does not include corrections for inflation or other factors that affect the true value of money in the future. This is used in time value of money calculations.

Exam Probability: **High**

2. *Answer choices:*

(see index for correct answer)

- a. QuantLib
- b. Business mathematics
- c. Financial correlation
- d. time consistent

Guidance: level 1

:: Underground culture ::

A black market, _____ , or shadow economy is a clandestine market or series of transactions that has some aspect of illegality or is characterized by some form of noncompliant behavior with an institutional set of rules. If the rule defines the set of goods and services whose production and distribution is prohibited by law, non-compliance with the rule constitutes a black market trade since the transaction itself is illegal. Parties engaging in the production or distribution of prohibited goods and services are members of the illegal economy. Examples include the drug trade, prostitution , illegal currency transactions and human trafficking. Violations of the tax code involving income tax evasion constitute membership in the unreported economy.

Exam Probability: **Medium**

3. *Answer choices:*

(see index for correct answer)

- a. Lolita City
- b. Peter Lamborn Wilson
- c. Animal Farm
- d. Underground economy

Guidance: level 1

:: Monetary reform ::

An _____ is an activity by a central bank to give liquidity in its currency to a bank or a group of banks. The central bank can either buy or sell government bonds in the open market or, in what is now mostly the preferred solution, enter into a repo or secured lending transaction with a commercial bank: the central bank gives the money as a deposit for a defined period and synchronously takes an eligible asset as collateral. A central bank uses OMO as the primary means of implementing monetary policy. The usual aim of _____ s is—aside from supplying commercial banks with liquidity and sometimes taking surplus liquidity from commercial banks—to manipulate the short-term interest rate and the supply of base money in an economy, and thus indirectly control the total money supply, in effect expanding money or contracting the money supply. This involves meeting the demand of base money at the target interest rate by buying and selling government securities, or other financial instruments. Monetary targets, such as inflation, interest rates, or exchange rates, are used to guide this implementation.

Exam Probability: **Medium**

4. *Answer choices:*

(see index for correct answer)

- a. Open market operation
- b. Mutual credit
- c. State bank
- d. A Program for Monetary Reform

Guidance: level 1

:: Finance ::

A _____ is a non-physical asset whose value is derived from a contractual claim, such as bank deposits, bonds, and stocks. _____s are usually more liquid than other tangible assets, such as commodities or real estate, and may be traded on financial markets.

Exam Probability: **Low**

5. *Answer choices:*

(see index for correct answer)

- a. Financial asset
- b. Negative return
- c. Finance
- d. Debt-for-nature swap

Guidance: level 1

:: Income distribution ::

In economics, _____ is how a nation's total GDP is distributed amongst its population. Income and its distribution have always been a central concern of economic theory and economic policy. Classical economists such as Adam Smith, Thomas Malthus, and David Ricardo were mainly concerned with factor _____ , that is, the distribution of income between the main factors of production, land, labour and capital. Modern economists have also addressed this issue, but have been more concerned with the distribution of income across individuals and households. Important theoretical and policy concerns include the balance between income inequality and economic growth, and their often inverse relationship.

6. *Answer choices:*

(see index for correct answer)

- a. M-shaped society
- b. Average is Over
- c. Income distribution
- d. Redistributive justice

Guidance: level 1

:: United States housing bubble ::

In economics, a _____ is a business cycle contraction when there is a general decline in economic activity. Macroeconomic indicators such as GDP , investment spending, capacity utilization, household income, business profits, and inflation fall, while bankruptcies and the unemployment rate rise. In the United Kingdom, it is defined as a negative economic growth for two consecutive quarters.

Exam Probability: **Medium**

7. *Answer choices:*

(see index for correct answer)

- a. Federal Housing Enterprises Financial Safety and Soundness Act of 1992

- b. Recession
- c. Shadow banking system
- d. Zombie title

Guidance: level 1

:: International taxation ::

A _____ is a tax on imports or exports between sovereign states. It is a form of regulation of foreign trade and a policy that taxes foreign products to encourage or safeguard domestic industry. _____ s are the simplest and oldest instrument of trade policy. Traditionally, states have used them as a source of income. Now, they are among the most widely used instruments of protection, along with import and export quotas.

Exam Probability: **High**

8. *Answer choices:*

(see index for correct answer)

- a. Withholding tax
- b. Tax equalization
- c. Tariff
- d. Inter-American Center of Tax Administrations

Guidance: level 1

:: National accounts ::

A _____ consists of one people who live in the same dwelling and share meals. It may also consist of a single family or another group of people. A dwelling is considered to contain multiple _____ s if meals or living spaces are not shared. The _____ is the basic unit of analysis in many social, microeconomic and government models, and is important to economics and inheritance.

Exam Probability: **Medium**

9. *Answer choices:*

(see index for correct answer)

- a. Household
- b. System of Environmental and Economic Accounting for Water
- c. War finance
- d. Compensation of employees

Guidance: level 1

:: Economics ::

An _____ is an area of the production, distribution, or trade, and consumption of goods and services by different agents. Understood in its broadest sense, `The _____ is defined as a social domain that emphasize the practices, discourses, and material expressions associated with the production, use, and management of resources`. Economic agents can be individuals, businesses, organizations, or governments. Economic transactions occur when two parties agree to the value or price of the transacted good or service, commonly expressed in a certain currency. However, monetary transactions only account for a small part of the economic domain.

Exam Probability: **High**

10. *Answer choices:*

(see index for correct answer)

- a. European Economic Senate
- b. Additionality
- c. Direct labour cost variance
- d. Economy

Guidance: level 1

:: Numismatics ::

_____ is a currency without intrinsic value that has been established as money, often by government regulation. _____ does not have use value, and has value only because a government maintains its value, or because parties engaging in exchange agree on its value. It was introduced as an alternative to commodity money and representative money. Commodity money is created from a good, often a precious metal such as gold or silver, which has uses other than as a medium of exchange . Representative money is similar to _____ , but it represents a claim on a commodity .

Exam Probability: **Low**

11. *Answer choices:*

(see index for correct answer)

- a. Guldengroschen
- b. Fiat money
- c. Centenionalis
- d. Orange Free State pound

Guidance: level 1

:: Accounting terminology ::

In financial accounting, a _____ or statement of financial position or statement of financial condition is a summary of the financial balances of an individual or organization, whether it be a sole proprietorship, a business partnership, a corporation, private limited company or other organization such as Government or not-for-profit entity. Assets, liabilities and ownership equity are listed as of a specific date, such as the end of its financial year. A _____ is often described as a "snapshot of a company's financial condition". Of the four basic financial statements, the _____ is the only statement which applies to a single point in time of a business' calendar year.

Exam Probability: **Low**

12. *Answer choices:*

(see index for correct answer)

- a. Accounts payable
- b. Matching principle
- c. Cash flow statement
- d. Balance sheet

Guidance: level 1

:: History of economic thought, methodology, and heterodox approaches ::

_____ is a part of economics that expresses value or normative judgments about economic fairness or what the outcome of the economy or goals of public policy ought to be.

13. *Answer choices:*

(see index for correct answer)

- a. Normative economics
- b. positive economics
- c. Feminist economics
- d. Schools of economic thought

Guidance: level 1

:: Committees ::

The _____ , a committee within the Federal Reserve System , is charged under United States law with overseeing the nation's open market operations . This Federal Reserve committee makes key decisions about interest rates and the growth of the United States money supply.

Exam Probability: **Low**

14. *Answer choices:*

(see index for correct answer)

- a. Treasury Board
- b. Committee on World Food Security
- c. Federal Open Market Committee

- d. Research-on-Research Committee

:: Standard of living ::

An individual's or a socioeconomic class's _____ is the level of wealth, comfort, material goods, and necessities available to them in a certain geographic area, usually a country. The _____ includes factors such as income, quality and availability of employment, class disparity, poverty rate, quality and affordability of housing, hours of work required to purchase necessities, gross domestic product, inflation rate, amount of leisure time every year, affordable access to quality healthcare, quality and availability of education, life expectancy, incidence of disease, cost of goods and services, infrastructure, national economic growth, economic and political stability,freedom, environmental quality, climate and safety. The _____ is closely related to quality of life.

Exam Probability: **High**

15. *Answer choices:*

(see index for correct answer)

- a. Standard of living in Japan
- b. Right to an adequate standard of living
- c. Standard of living in the United States
- d. Standard of living

:: Films based on financial crisis ::

_____ is an eight-block-long street running roughly northwest to southeast from Broadway to South Street, at the East River, in the Financial District of Lower Manhattan in New York City. Over time, the term has become a metonym for the financial markets of the United States as a whole, the American financial services industry , or New York–based financial interests.

Exam Probability: **High**

16. *Answer choices:*

(see index for correct answer)

- a. The Roaring Twenties
- b. The Crash
- c. Ilo Ilo
- d. Money for Nothing: Inside the Federal Reserve

Guidance: level 1

:: Financial economics ::

The reserve requirement is a central bank regulation employed by most, but not all, of the world's central banks, that sets the minimum amount of reserves that must be held by a commercial bank. The minimum reserve is generally determined by the central bank to be no less than a specified percentage of the amount of deposit liabilities the commercial bank owes to its customers. The commercial bank's reserves normally consist of cash owned by the bank and stored physically in the bank vault , plus the amount of the commercial bank's balance in that bank's account with the central bank.

Exam Probability: **Medium**

17. *Answer choices:*

(see index for correct answer)

- a. Required reserve ratio
- b. Required reserves
- c. Added value
- d. Deutsche Bank Prize in Financial Economics

Guidance: level 1

:: Money ::

In economics, _____ is money in the physical form of currency, such as banknotes and coins. In bookkeeping and finance, _____ is current assets comprising currency or currency equivalents that can be accessed immediately or near-immediately . _____ is seen either as a reserve for payments, in case of a structural or incidental negative _____ flow or as a way to avoid a downturn on financial markets.

18. *Answer choices:*

(see index for correct answer)

- a. Millionaire
- b. Rai stones
- c. Token money
- d. Commodity money

Guidance: level 1

:: Microeconomics ::

In economics, _____ , resources, or inputs are what is used in the production process to produce output—that is, finished goods and services. The utilized amounts of the various inputs determine the quantity of output according to the relationship called the production function. There are three basic resources or _____ : land, labor, and capital. The factors are also frequently labeled "producer goods or services" to distinguish them from the goods or services purchased by consumers, which are frequently labeled "consumer goods".

Exam Probability: **High**

19. *Answer choices:*

(see index for correct answer)

- a. Factors of production
- b. Shutdown
- c. Contour set
- d. Hoarding

Guidance: level 1

:: Fixed income market ::

The _____ is a financial market where participants can issue new debt, known as the primary market, or buy and sell debt securities, known as the secondary market. This is usually in the form of bonds, but it may include notes, bills, and so on.

Exam Probability: **Low**

20. *Answer choices:*

(see index for correct answer)

- a. Bond Exchange of South Africa
- b. Fixed income
- c. Fixed-income attribution
- d. Bond market

Guidance: level 1

:: Great Depression ::

The _____ was a severe worldwide economic depression that took place mostly during the 1930s, beginning in the United States. The timing of the _____ varied across nations; in most countries it started in 1929 and lasted until the late-1930s. It was the longest, deepest, and most widespread depression of the 20th century. In the 21st century, the _____ is commonly used as an example of how intensely the world's economy can decline.

Exam Probability: **Low**

21. *Answer choices:*

(see index for correct answer)

- a. Yanks for Stalin
- b. Great Compression
- c. Sales tax token
- d. Causes of the Great Depression

Guidance: level 1

:: Goods ::

In economics, a _____ is a good that is both non-excludable and non-rivalrous in that individuals cannot be excluded from use or could be enjoyed without paying for it, and where use by one individual does not reduce availability to others or the goods can be effectively consumed simultaneously by more than one person. This is in contrast to a common good which is non-excludable but is rivalrous to a certain degree.

Exam Probability: **High**

22. *Answer choices:*

(see index for correct answer)

- a. Global public good
- b. Independent goods
- c. Public good
- d. Durable good

Guidance: level 1

:: Valuation (finance) ::

The _____ is one of three major groups of methodologies, called valuation approaches, used by appraisers. It is particularly common in commercial real estate appraisal and in business appraisal. The fundamental math is similar to the methods used for financial valuation, securities analysis, or bond pricing. However, there are some significant and important modifications when used in real estate or business valuation.

23. *Answer choices:*

(see index for correct answer)

- a. Channel check
- b. Income approach
- c. Financial analysis
- d. Diminution in value

Guidance: level 1

:: Microeconomics ::

An _____ is a contingent motivator. Traditional _____ s are extrinsic motivators which reward actions to yield a desired outcome. The effectiveness of traditional _____ s has changed as the needs of Western society have evolved. While the traditional _____ model is effective when there is a defined procedure and goal for a task, Western society started to require a higher volume of critical thinkers, so the traditional model became less effective. Institutions are now following a trend in implementing strategies that rely on intrinsic motivations rather than the extrinsic motivations that the traditional _____ s foster.

Exam Probability: **Medium**

24. *Answer choices:*

(see index for correct answer)

- a. Transaction cost
- b. Economies of scope
- c. In kind
- d. Incentive

Guidance: level 1

:: Economics terminology ::

In economics, _____ or just capital is a factor of production , consisting of machinery, buildings, computers, and the like. The production function takes the general form Y=f, where Y is the amount of output produced, K is the amount of capital stock used, L is the amount of labor used, and N is the amount of natural resources used. In economic theory, _____ is one of the three primary factors of production; the others are natural resources , and laborthe stock of competences embodied in the labor force. _____ is distinct from human capital , circulating capital, and financial capital. _____ is fixed capital, which is any kind of real physical asset that is not used up in the production of a product. Usually the value of land is not included in _____ as it is not a reproducible product of human activities.

Exam Probability: **High**

25. *Answer choices:*

(see index for correct answer)

- a. Exit
- b. equation of exchange

- c. Wage dispersion
- d. Physical capital

Guidance: level 1

:: Monetary economics ::

_____ are a commercial bank's holdings of deposits in accounts with a central bank , plus currency that is physically held in the bank's vault . Some central banks set minimum reserve requirements, which require banks to hold deposits at the central bank equivalent to at least a specified percentage of their liabilities such as customer deposits. Even when there are no reserve requirements, banks often opt to hold some reserves—called desired reserves—against unexpected events such as unusually large net withdrawals by customers or bank runs.

Exam Probability: **Low**

26. *Answer choices:*
(see index for correct answer)

- a. Monetary equilibrium
- b. Fiscal theory of the price level
- c. Coincidence of wants
- d. Bank reserves

Guidance: level 1

:: Economic problems ::

The causes of _____ are heavily debated. Classical economics, new classical economics, and the Austrian School of economics argued that market mechanisms are reliable means of resolving _____ . These theories argue against interventions imposed on the labor market from the outside, such as unionization, bureaucratic work rules, minimum wage laws, taxes, and other regulations that they claim discourage the hiring of workers. Keynesian economics emphasizes the cyclical nature of _____ and recommends government interventions in the economy that it claims will reduce _____ during recessions. This theory focuses on recurrent shocks that suddenly reduce aggregate demand for goods and services and thus reduce demand for workers. Keynesian models recommend government interventions designed to increase demand for workers; these can include financial stimuli, publicly funded job creation, and expansionist monetary policies. Its namesake economist, John Maynard Keynes, believed that the root cause of _____ is the desire of investors to receive more money rather than produce more products, which is not possible without public bodies producing new money. A third group of theories emphasize the need for a stable supply of capital and investment to maintain full employment. On this view, government should guarantee full employment through fiscal policy, monetary policy and trade policy as stated, for example, in the US Employment Act of 1946, by counteracting private sector or trade investment volatility, and reducing inequality.

Exam Probability: **High**

27. *Answer choices:*

(see index for correct answer)

- a. Sub-replacement fertility
- b. Bank Transfer Day
- c. Overcapitalisation
- d. Middle-class squeeze

:: Welfare economics ::

Unemployment benefits are payments made by back authorized bodies to unemployed people. In the United States, benefits are funded by a compulsory governmental insurance system, not taxes on individual citizens. Depending on the jurisdiction and the status of the person, those sums may be small, covering only basic needs, or may compensate the lost time proportionally to the previous earned salary.

Exam Probability: **High**

28. *Answer choices:*

(see index for correct answer)

- a. Laeken indicators
- b. Wikiprogress
- c. Unemployment insurance
- d. Social welfare function

:: International trade ::

An _____ is a type of trade restriction that sets a physical limit on the quantity of a good that can be imported into a country in a given period of time.

Exam Probability: **Medium**

29. *Answer choices:*

(see index for correct answer)

- a. African Diamond Producers Association
- b. Certificate of Formula Compliance
- c. Ocean freight differential
- d. Import quota

Guidance: level 1

:: Economics terminology ::

The law or principle of _____ holds that under free trade, an agent will produce more of and consume less of a good for which they have a _____ . _____ is the economic reality describing the work gains from trade for individuals, firms, or nations, which arise from differences in their factor endowments or technological progress. In an economic model, agents have a _____ over others in producing a particular good if they can produce that good at a lower relative opportunity cost or autarky price, i.e. at a lower relative marginal cost prior to trade. One shouldn`t compare the monetary costs of production or even the resource costs of production. Instead, one must compare the opportunity costs of producing goods across countries.

30. *Answer choices:*

- a. Decommercialization
- b. Comparative advantage
- c. Extensive growth
- d. discrete choice model

Guidance: level 1

:: Rational choice theory ::

In economics, " _____ " are model-consistent expectations, in that agents inside the model are assumed to "know the model" and on average take the model's predictions as valid. _____ ensure internal consistency in models involving uncertainty. To obtain consistency within a model, the predictions of future values of economically relevant variables from the model are assumed to be the same as that of the decision-makers in the model, given their information set, the nature of the random processes involved, and model structure. The _____ assumption is used especially in many contemporary macroeconomic models.

31. *Answer choices:*

- a. The Logic of Collective Action
- b. Trade-off talking rational economic person
- c. Rational expectations
- d. Social Choice and Individual Values

Guidance: level 1

:: Economics ::

_____ is the social science that studies the production, distribution, and consumption of goods and services.

Exam Probability: **High**

32. *Answer choices:*

(see index for correct answer)

- a. Financial compensation
- b. Direct labour cost variance
- c. Cash collection
- d. Additionality

Guidance: level 1

:: Public finance ::

_____ or expenditure includes all government consumption, investment, and transfer payments. In national income accounting the acquisition by governments of goods and services for current use, to directly satisfy the individual or collective needs of the community, is classed as government final consumption expenditure. Government acquisition of goods and services intended to create future benefits, such as infrastructure investment or research spending, is classed as government investment . These two types of _____, on final consumption and on gross capital formation, together constitute one of the major components of gross domestic product.

Exam Probability: **Low**

33. *Answer choices:*

(see index for correct answer)

- a. Tax revenue
- b. Unitax
- c. Government spending
- d. Great Lakes Higher Education Corporation

Guidance: level 1

:: Macroeconomics ::

A _____ is an event that suddenly increases or decreases the supply of a commodity or service, or of commodities and services in general. This sudden change affects the equilibrium price of the good or service or the economy's general price level.

34. *Answer choices:*

(see index for correct answer)

- a. Microsimulation
- b. Demand shock
- c. Overheating
- d. Supply shock

Guidance: level 1

:: Economics curves ::

The _____ is a single-equation econometric model, named after WilliamPhillips, describing a historical inverse relationship between rates of unemployment and corresponding rates of rises in wages that result within an economy. Stated simply, decreased unemployment, in an economy will correlate with higher rates of wage rises. Phillips did not himself state there was any relationship between employment and inflation; this notion was a trivial deduction from his statistical findings. Samuelson and Solow made the connection explicit and subsequently Milton Friedman and Edmund Phelpsput the theoretical structure in place. In so doing, Friedman was to successfully predict the imminent collapse of Phillips` a-theoretic correlation.

Exam Probability: **Medium**

35. *Answer choices:*

(see index for correct answer)

- a. Demand curve
- b. Phillips curve
- c. Yield curve
- d. Hubbert curve

Guidance: level 1

:: Markets (customer bases) ::

In economics, _____ is the economic price for which a good or service is offered in the marketplace. It is of interest mainly in the study of microeconomics. Market value and _____ are equal only under conditions of market efficiency, equilibrium, and rational expectations.

Exam Probability: **High**

36. *Answer choices:*

(see index for correct answer)

- a. Market system
- b. Market price
- c. market equilibrium
- d. Nonmarket

Guidance: level 1

:: Macroeconomic policy ::

In macroeconomics, _____ s are features of the structure of modern government budgets, particularly income taxes and welfare spending, that act to dampen fluctuations in real GDP.

Exam Probability: **High**

37. *Answer choices:*

(see index for correct answer)

- a. Automatic stabilizer
- b. Lucas critique
- c. General maximum
- d. Automatic stabilizers

Guidance: level 1

:: United States housing bubble ::

In finance, _____ lending means making loans to people who may have difficulty maintaining the repayment schedule, sometimes reflecting setbacks, such as unemployment, divorce, medical emergencies, etc. Historically, _____ borrowers were defined as having FICO scores below 600, although "this has varied over time and circumstances."

Exam Probability: **High**

38. *Answer choices:*

- a. Subprime
- b. Flipping
- c. Libor
- d. secondary mortgage market

Guidance: level 1

:: Microeconomics ::

A _____ is the price of a commodity such as a good or service in terms of another; i.e., the ratio of two prices. A _____ may be expressed in terms of a ratio between the prices of any two goods or the ratio between the price of one good and the price of a market basket of goods . A _____ is an opportunity cost. Microeconomics can be seen as the study of how economic agents react to changes in _____ s, and of how _____ s are affected by the behavior of those agents.

Exam Probability: **High**

39. *Answer choices:*

- a. Product proliferation
- b. Isocost
- c. Repugnancy costs

- d. Relative price

Guidance: level 1

:: Export ::

An _____ in international trade is a good or service produced in one country that is bought by someone in another country. The seller of such goods and services is an _____ er; the foreign buyer is an importer.

Exam Probability: **Low**

40. *Answer choices:*

(see index for correct answer)

- a. Live export
- b. Export
- c. Export variants of Soviet military equipment

Guidance: level 1

:: International economics ::

In economics, the principle of _____ refers to the ability of a party to produce a greater quantity of a good, product, or service than competitors, using the same amount of resources. Adam Smith first described the principle of _____ in the context of international trade, using labor as the only input. Since _____ is determined by a simple comparison of labor productiveness, it is possible for a party to have no _____ in anything.

Exam Probability: **Low**

41. *Answer choices:*

(see index for correct answer)

- a. David Ricardo
- b. Absolute advantage
- c. Atlas method
- d. Sovereign wealth fund

Guidance: level 1

:: Economics terminology ::

_____ is the process by which the money supply of a country, or of an economic or monetary region, is increased. In most modern economies, most of the money supply is in the form of bank deposits. Central banks monitor the amount of money in the economy by measuring the so-called monetary aggregates.

Exam Probability: **High**

42. *Answer choices:*

(see index for correct answer)

- a. Money creation
- b. Sampo generation
- c. Market cannibalism
- d. Headcount ratio

Guidance: level 1

:: Dividends ::

A _____ is a payment made by a corporation to its shareholders, usually as a distribution of profits. When a corporation earns a profit or surplus, the corporation is able to re-invest the profit in the business and pay a proportion of the profit as a _____ to shareholders. Distribution to shareholders may be in cash or, if the corporation has a _____ reinvestment plan, the amount can be paid by the issue of further shares or share repurchase. When _____ s are paid, shareholders typically must pay income taxes, and the corporation does not receive a corporate income tax deduction for the _____ payments.

Exam Probability: **Low**

43. *Answer choices:*

(see index for correct answer)

- a. Dividend
- b. Dividend future

- c. Division 7A dividend
- d. Liquidating distribution

Guidance: level 1

:: Financial markets ::

_____ or OMV is the price at which an asset would trade in a competitive auction setting. _____ is often used interchangeably with open _____ , fair value or fair _____ , although these terms have distinct definitions in different standards, and may or may not differ in some circumstances.

Exam Probability: **Low**

44. *Answer choices:*

(see index for correct answer)

- a. Flight-to-liquidity
- b. Market value
- c. Intermarket analysis
- d. Big boy letter

Guidance: level 1

:: Asymmetric information ::

In economics, _____ occurs when someone increases their exposure to risk when insured, especially when a person takes more risks because someone else bears the cost of those risks. A _____ may occur where the actions of one party may change to the detriment of another after a financial transaction has taken place.

Exam Probability: **Medium**

45. *Answer choices:*

(see index for correct answer)

- a. Pooling equilibrium
- b. Moral hazard
- c. Principal
- d. Single-crossing

Guidance: level 1

:: Banking ::

A _____ or term deposit is an interest-bearing bank deposit with a specified period of maturity. It is a money deposit at a banking institution that cannot be withdrawn for a specific term or period of time . When the term is over, it can be either withdrawn or held for another term. Generally speaking, the longer the term, the better the yield on the money.

Exam Probability: **High**

46. *Answer choices:*

(see index for correct answer)

- a. Giro
- b. Prize-Linked Savings Account
- c. Bank secrecy
- d. Deposit market share

Guidance: level 1

:: Separation of investment and commercial banking ::

A _____ is a type of bank that provides services such as accepting deposits, making business loans, and offering basic investment products that is operated as a business for profit.

Exam Probability: **Low**

47. *Answer choices:*

(see index for correct answer)

- a. speculation
- b. Commercial bank
- c. Retail banking
- d. Bancassurance

Guidance: level 1

:: International economics ::

A _____ , sometimes called a pegged exchange rate, is a type of exchange rate regime in which a currency's value is fixed against either the value of another single currency, a basket of other currencies, or another measure of value, such as gold.

Exam Probability: **Low**

48. *Answer choices:*

(see index for correct answer)

- a. Fixed exchange rate
- b. World Integrated Trade Solution
- c. Net international investment position
- d. Outsourcing

Guidance: level 1

:: Investment ::

An _____ is a mutual fund or exchange-traded fund designed to follow certain preset rules so that the fund can track a specified basket of underlying investments. Those rules may include tracking prominent indexes like the S&P 500 or the Dow Jones Industrial Average or implementation rules, such as tax-management, tracking error minimization, large block trading or patient/flexible trading strategies that allows for greater tracking error, but lower market impact costs. _____ s may also have rules that screen for social and sustainable criteria.

Exam Probability: **High**

49. *Answer choices:*

(see index for correct answer)

- a. Index fund
- b. inventory investment
- c. Capital market line
- d. Value Research

Guidance: level 1

:: Government bonds ::

A _____ or sovereign bond is a bond issued by a national government, generally with a promise to pay periodic interest payments called coupon payments and to repay the face value on the maturity date. The aim of a _____ is to support government spending. _____ s are usually denominated in the country's own currency, in which case the government cannot be forced to default, although it may choose to do so. If a government is close to default on its debt the media often refer to this as a sovereign debt crisis.

Exam Probability: **Medium**

50. *Answer choices:*

(see index for correct answer)

- a. Texas v. White
- b. Municipal bond
- c. Eurobonds
- d. Government bond

Guidance: level 1

:: Central banks ::

A _____ , reserve bank, or monetary authority is the institution that manages the currency, money supply, and interest rates of a state or formal monetary union,and oversees their commercial banking system. In contrast to a commercial bank, a _____ possesses a monopoly on increasing the monetary base in the state, and also generally controls the printing/coining of the national currency, which serves as the state's legal tender. A _____ also acts as a lender of last resort to the banking sector during times of financial crisis. Most _____ s also have supervisory and regulatory powers to ensure the solvency of member institutions, to prevent bank runs, and to discourage reckless or fraudulent behavior by member banks.

Exam Probability: **High**

51. *Answer choices:*

(see index for correct answer)

- a. National Bank of the Kyrgyz Republic
- b. Central bank
- c. Bank of Japan
- d. Central Bank of Liberia

Guidance: level 1

:: Financial markets ::

In economics and finance, _____ is the practice of taking advantage of a price difference between two or more markets: striking a combination of matching deals that capitalize upon the imbalance, the profit being the difference between the market prices. When used by academics, an _____ is a transaction that involves no negative cash flow at any probabilistic or temporal state and a positive cash flow in at least one state; in simple terms, it is the possibility of a risk-free profit after transaction costs. For example, an _____ opportunity is present when there is the opportunity to instantaneously buy something for a low price and sell it for a higher price.

Exam Probability: **High**

52. *Answer choices:*

(see index for correct answer)

- a. Fution
- b. Market depth
- c. Financial market
- d. Power Plus Pro

Guidance: level 1

:: United States Department of Commerce agencies ::

The _____ of the United States Department of Commerce is a U.S. government agency that provides official macroeconomic and industry statistics, most notably reports about the gross domestic product of the United States and its various units—states, cities/towns/townships/villages/counties and metropolitan areas. They also provide information about personal income, corporate profits, and government spending in their National Income and Product Accounts .

Exam Probability: **High**

53. *Answer choices:*

(see index for correct answer)

- a. National Telecommunications and Information Administration
- b. Economics and Statistics Administration
- c. United States Commercial Service
- d. National Oceanographic Data Center

Guidance: level 1

:: Price controls ::

A _____ is a government- or group-imposed price control or limit on how low a price can be charged for a product, good, commodity, or service. A _____ must be higher than the equilibrium price in order to be effective. The equilibrium price, commonly called the "market price", is the price where economic forces such as supply and demand are balanced and in the absence of external influences the values of economic variables will not change, often described as the point at which quantity demanded and quantity supplied are equal . Governments use _____ s to keep certain prices from going too low.

Exam Probability: **Low**

54. *Answer choices:*

(see index for correct answer)

- a. Administered price
- b. Price support
- c. Price floor
- d. Flour War

Guidance: level 1

:: Financial economics ::

The reserve requirement is a central bank regulation employed by most, but not all, of the world`s central banks, that sets the minimum amount of reserves that must be held by a commercial bank. The minimum reserve is generally determined by the central bank to be no less than a specified percentage of the amount of deposit liabilities the commercial bank owes to its customers. The commercial bank`s reserves normally consist of cash owned by the bank and stored physically in the bank vault , plus the amount of the commercial bank`s balance in that bank`s account with the central bank.

Exam Probability: **High**

55. *Answer choices:*

(see index for correct answer)

- a. Prime rate
- b. Information coefficient
- c. Reserve ratio
- d. MarHedge

Guidance: level 1

:: Business cycle ::

An _____ is the phase of the business cycle following a recession, during which an economy regains and exceeds peak employment and output levels achieved prior to downturn. A recovery period is typically characterized by abnormally high levels of growth in real gross domestic product, employment, corporate profits, and other indicators.

56. *Answer choices:*

(see index for correct answer)

- a. Business cycle
- b. Trough
- c. Economic recovery
- d. Economic Confidence Model

Guidance: level 1

:: Warrants issued in Hong Kong Stock Exchange ::

The _____ is the official currency of 19 of the 28 member states of
the _____ pean Union. This group of states is known as the _____ zone
or _____ area, and counts about 343 million citizens as of 2019. The
_____ is the second largest and second most traded currency in the foreign
exchange market after the United States dollar. The _____ is divided into
100 cents.

Exam Probability: **High**

57. *Answer choices:*

(see index for correct answer)

- a. Bank of Communications
- b. Tencent

- c. Euro
- d. Dongfang Electric

Guidance: level 1

:: Generally Accepted Accounting Principles ::

The _____ of a corporation is the accumulated net income of the corporation that is retained by the corporation at a particular point of time, such as at the end of the reporting period. At the end of that period, the net income at that point is transferred from the Profit and Loss Account to the _____ account. If the balance of the _____ account is negative it may be called accumulated losses, retained losses or accumulated deficit, or similar terminology.

Exam Probability: **Low**

58. *Answer choices:*

(see index for correct answer)

- a. Fixed asset
- b. Normal balance
- c. Retained earnings
- d. Paid in capital

Guidance: level 1

:: Socialism ::

The _____ Union, officially the Union of _____ Socialist Republics , was a socialist state in Eurasia that existed from 1922 to 1991. Nominally a union of multiple national _____ republics, its government and economy were highly centralized. The country was a one-party state, governed by the Communist Party with Moscow as its capital in its largest republic, the Russian _____ Federative Socialist Republic . Other major urban centres were Leningrad, Kiev, Minsk, Alma-Ata, and Novosibirsk. It spanned over 10,000 kilometres east to west across 11 time zones, and over 7,200 kilometres north to south. It had five climate zones: tundra, taiga, steppes, desert and mountains.

Exam Probability: **Medium**

59. *Answer choices:*

(see index for correct answer)

- a. Is There for Honest Poverty
- b. Arab socialism
- c. Pink tide
- d. Nanosocialism

Guidance: level 1

Business economics

Business economics is a field in applied economics which uses economic theory and quantitative methods to analyze business enterprises and the factors contributing to the diversity of organizational structures and the relationships of firms with labour, capital and product markets.

:: Derivatives (finance) ::

A _____ or futures market is a central financial exchange where people can trade standardized futures contracts; that is, a contract to buy specific quantities of a commodity or financial instrument at a specified price with delivery set at a specified time in the future. These types of contracts fall into the category of derivatives. The opposite of the futures market is the spots market, where trades will occur immediately after a transaction agreement has been made, rather than at a predetermined time in the future. Futures instruments are priced according to the movement of the underlying asset . The aforementioned category is named "derivatives" because the value of these instruments are derived from another asset class.

Exam Probability: **Medium**

1. *Answer choices:*

(see index for correct answer)

- a. Futures exchange
- b. Notional amount
- c. ISDA Master Agreement
- d. Delivery month

Guidance: level 1

:: Separation of investment and commercial banking ::

A _____ is a type of bank that provides services such as accepting deposits, making business loans, and offering basic investment products that is operated as a business for profit.

2. *Answer choices:*

(see index for correct answer)

- a. Commercial bank
- b. Independent Commission on Banking
- c. investment banks
- d. Universal bank

Guidance: level 1

:: Credit ::

A _____ occurs when a person or organization defaults on a significant transaction. He or she is unable to honor the terms of the contract entered, and the borrower's ability to pay comes into question. Because the marketplace recognizes such events as related to one's credit worthiness, _____ s can trigger specific protections provided by credit derivatives .

3. *Answer choices:*

(see index for correct answer)

- a. Credit fracking
- b. Credit event

- c. Loan covenant
- d. Quizzle

Guidance: level 1

:: Financial risk ::

In finance and economics, _____ is vulnerability to events which affect aggregate outcomes such as broad market returns, total economy-wide resource holdings, or aggregate income. In many contexts, events like earthquakes and major weather catastrophes pose aggregate risks that affect not only the distribution but also the total amount of resources. If every possible outcome of a stochastic economic process is characterized by the same aggregate result , the process then has no aggregate risk.

Exam Probability: **Medium**

4. *Answer choices:*

(see index for correct answer)

- a. Dogs of the Dow
- b. Coherent risk measure
- c. Superhedging price
- d. Institute of Operational Risk

Guidance: level 1

:: Foreign exchange market ::

The _____ is a hypothesis in international finance that suggests differences in nominal interest rates reflect expected changes in the spot exchange rate between countries. The hypothesis specifically states that a spot exchange rate is expected to change equally in the opposite direction of the interest rate differential; thus, the currency of the country with the higher nominal interest rate is expected to depreciate against the currency of the country with the lower nominal interest rate, as higher nominal interest rates reflect an expectation of inflation.

Exam Probability: **Low**

5. *Answer choices:*

(see index for correct answer)

- a. Billion Dollar Day
- b. Exchange-rate regime
- c. Global-View.com
- d. International Fisher effect

Guidance: level 1

:: International economics ::

In finance, an _____ is the rate at which one currency will be exchanged for another. It is also regarded as the value of one country's currency in relation to another currency. For example, an interbank _____ of 114 Japanese yen to the United States dollar means that ¥114 will be exchanged for each US$1 or that US$1 will be exchanged for each ¥114. In this case it is said that the price of a dollar in relation to yen is ¥114, or equivalently that the price of a yen in relation to dollars is $1/114.

Exam Probability: **High**

6. *Answer choices:*

(see index for correct answer)

- a. Exchange rate
- b. Padala
- c. Bureau de change
- d. Dutch disease

Guidance: level 1

:: E-commerce ::

A _____ is a plastic payment card that can be used instead of cash when making purchases. It is similar to a credit card, but unlike a credit card, the money is immediately transferred directly from the cardholder's bank account when performing a transaction.

Exam Probability: **Medium**

7. *Answer choices:*

(see index for correct answer)

- a. Blind credential
- b. Webjet
- c. Online flower delivery
- d. Friend-to-friend

Guidance: level 1

:: Finance theories ::

The _____ is a method of valuing a company's stock price based on the theory that its stock is worth the sum of all of its future dividend payments, discounted back to their present value. In other words, it is used to value stocks based on the net present value of the future dividends. The equation most widely used is called the Gordon growth model . It is named after Myron J. Gordon of the University of Toronto, who originally published it along with Eli Shapiro in 1956 and made reference to it in 1959. Their work borrowed heavily from the theoretical and mathematical ideas found in John Burr Williams 1938 book "The Theory of Investment Value."

Exam Probability: **Low**

8. *Answer choices:*

(see index for correct answer)

- a. Black model
- b. Dividend discount model

- c. Consumption-based capital asset pricing model
- d. Martingale pricing

Guidance: level 1

:: Financial markets ::

In economics, _____ is the process by which, in an economic market, the supply of whatever is traded is equated to the demand, so that there is no leftover supply or demand. The new classical economics assumes that, in any given market, assuming that all buyers and sellers have access to information and that there is not "friction" impeding price changes, prices always adjust up or down to ensure _____ .

Exam Probability: **High**

9. *Answer choices:*

(see index for correct answer)

- a. FIXatdl
- b. Power Plus Pro
- c. Mid price
- d. Market clearing

Guidance: level 1

:: Goods ::

In economics, a _____ is a good that is both non-excludable and non-rivalrous in that individuals cannot be excluded from use or could be enjoyed without paying for it, and where use by one individual does not reduce availability to others or the goods can be effectively consumed simultaneously by more than one person. This is in contrast to a common good which is non-excludable but is rivalrous to a certain degree.

Exam Probability: **Medium**

10. *Answer choices:*

(see index for correct answer)

- a. Fast-moving consumer goods
- b. Search good
- c. Common good
- d. Public good

Guidance: level 1

:: Industrial organization ::

In economics, _____ or industrial economy is a field that builds on the theory of the firm by examining the structure of firms and markets. _____ adds real-world complications to the perfectly competitive model, complications such as transaction costs, limited information, and barriers to entry of new firms that may be associated with imperfect competition. It analyzes determinants of firm and market organization and behavior as between competition and monopoly, including from government actions.

11. *Answer choices:*

(see index for correct answer)

- a. Tapered integration
- b. Limit pricing
- c. Hold-up problem
- d. Industrial inertia

Guidance: level 1

:: Agricultural economics ::

_____ is an applied field of economics concerned with the application of economic theory in optimizing the production and distribution of food and fiber. _____ began as a branch of economics that specifically dealt with land usage, it focused on maximizing the crop yield while maintaining a good soil ecosystem. Throughout the 20th century the discipline expanded and the current scope of the discipline is much broader. _____ today includes a variety of applied areas, having considerable overlap with conventional economics. Agricultural economists have made substantial contributions to research in economics, econometrics, development economics, and environmental economics. _____ influences food policy, agricultural policy, and environmental policy.

Exam Probability: **Medium**

12. *Answer choices:*

(see index for correct answer)

- a. Journal of Agricultural Economics
- b. Farmers Weekly
- c. CAPRI model
- d. Agricultural economics

Guidance: level 1

:: Property ::

_____ , in the abstract, is what belongs to or with something, whether as an attribute or as a component of said thing. In the context of this article, it is one or more components , whether physical or incorporeal, of a person's estate; or so belonging to, as in being owned by, a person or jointly a group of people or a legal entity like a corporation or even a society. Depending on the nature of the _____ , an owner of _____ has the right to consume, alter, share, redefine, rent, mortgage, pawn, sell, exchange, transfer, give away or destroy it, or to exclude others from doing these things, as well as to perhaps abandon it; whereas regardless of the nature of the _____ , the owner thereof has the right to properly use it , or at the very least exclusively keep it.

Exam Probability: **High**

13. *Answer choices:*
(see index for correct answer)

- a. Rack-rent

- b. Lost and found
- c. Sarf-e-Khas
- d. Counter-mapping

Guidance: level 1

:: Microeconomics ::

In economics, an _____ connects points on a graph representing different quantities of two goods, points between which a consumer is indifferent. That is, the consumer has no preference for one combination or bundle of goods over a different combination on the same curve. One can also refer to each point on the _____ as rendering the same level of utility for the consumer. In other words, an _____ is the locus of various points showing different combinations of two goods providing equal utility to the consumer. Utility is then a device to represent preferences rather than something from which preferences come. The main use of _____ s is in the representation of potentially observable demand patterns for individual consumers over commodity bundles.

Exam Probability: **High**

14. *Answer choices:*

(see index for correct answer)

- a. Total cost of ownership
- b. Overchoice
- c. In kind
- d. Indifference curve

:: Macroeconomics ::

_____ s is a branch of economics dealing with the performance, structure, behavior, and decision-making of an economy as a whole. This includes regional, national, and global economies. Macroeconomists study aggregated indicators such as GDP, unemployment rates, national income, price indices, and the interrelations among the different sectors of the economy to better understand how the whole economy functions. They also develop models that explain the relationship between such factors as national income, output, consumption, unemployment, inflation, saving, investment, international trade, and international finance.

Exam Probability: **High**

15. *Answer choices:*

(see index for correct answer)

- a. Macroeconomic policy instruments
- b. Macroeconomic
- c. Adaptive expectations
- d. Float

:: Financial ratios ::

In accounting, the _____ is a measure of the number of times inventory is sold or used in a time period such as a year. It is calculated to see if a business has an excessive inventory in comparison to its sales level. The equation for _____ equals the cost of goods sold divided by the average inventory. _____ is also known as inventory turns, merchandise turnover, stockturn, stock turns, turns, and stock turnover.

Exam Probability: **Low**

16. *Answer choices:*

(see index for correct answer)

- a. Accounting rate of return
- b. Average propensity to consume
- c. Earnings yield
- d. Inventory turnover

Guidance: level 1

:: Resource economics ::

A _____ is a source or supply from which a benefit is produced and it has some utility. _____ s can broadly be classified upon their availability—they are classified into renewable and non-renewable _____ s.Examples of non renewable _____ s are coal ,crude oil natural gas nuclear energy etc. Examples of renewable _____ s are air,water,wind,solar energy etc. They can also be classified as actual and potential on the basis of level of development and use, on the basis of origin they can be classified as biotic and abiotic, and on the basis of their distribution, as ubiquitous and localized . An item becomes a _____ with time and developing technology. Typically, _____ s are materials, energy, services, staff, knowledge, or other assets that are transformed to produce benefit and in the process may be consumed or made unavailable. Benefits of _____ utilization may include increased wealth, proper functioning of a system, or enhanced well-being. From a human perspective a natural _____ is anything obtained from the environment to satisfy human needs and wants. From a broader biological or ecological perspective a _____ satisfies the needs of a living organism .

Exam Probability: **Low**

17. *Answer choices:*

(see index for correct answer)

- a. Bioeconomics
- b. Material flow
- c. Material flow accounting
- d. Resource

Guidance: level 1

:: Mathematical finance ::

The _____ in financial mathematics and economics estimates the relationship between nominal and real interest rates under inflation. It is named after Irving Fisher, who was famous for his works on the theory of interest. In finance, the _____ is primarily used in YTM calculations of bonds or IRR calculations of investments. In economics, this equation is used to predict nominal and real interest rate behavior.

Exam Probability: **High**

18. *Answer choices:*
(see index for correct answer)

- a. Financial correlation
- b. Financial engineering
- c. Fisher equation
- d. Weighted average cost of capital

Guidance: level 1

:: Foreign direct investment ::

_____ s are residency-based measures such as transaction taxes, other limits, or outright prohibitions that a nation's government can use to regulate flows from capital markets into and out of the country's capital account. These measures may be economy-wide, sector-specific , or industry specific . They may apply to all flows, or may differentiate by type or duration of the flow .

Exam Probability: **High**

19. *Answer choices:*

(see index for correct answer)

- a. Capital control
- b. Foreign exchange controls
- c. Immigrant investor programs
- d. Expropriation

Guidance: level 1

:: Organizational theory ::

Decentralisation is the process by which the activities of an organization, particularly those regarding planning and decision making, are distributed or delegated away from a central, authoritative location or group. Concepts of _____ have been applied to group dynamics and management science in private businesses and organizations, political science, law and public administration, economics, money and technology.

Exam Probability: **Low**

20. *Answer choices:*

(see index for correct answer)

- a. Organisational semiotics
- b. Decentralization
- c. Sociogram
- d. Linking pin model

:: Financial risk ::

In finance, _____ is the risk of loss resulting from using insufficiently accurate models to make decisions, originally and frequently in the context of valuing financial securities. However, _____ is more and more prevalent in activities other than financial securities valuation, such as assigning consumer credit scores, real-time probability prediction of fraudulent credit card transactions, and computing the probability of air flight passenger being a terrorist. Rebonato in 2002 defines _____ as "the risk of occurrence of a significant difference between the mark-to-model value of a complex and/or illiquid instrument, and the price at which the same instrument is revealed to have traded in the market".

Exam Probability: **High**

21. *Answer choices:*

(see index for correct answer)

- a. Expected loss
- b. Five risks
- c. Credit scorecards
- d. Model risk

:: Corporate finance ::

In finance, a _____ is an investment transaction by which the ownership equity of a company, or a majority share of the stock of the company is acquired. The acquiror thereby "buys out" the present equity holders of the target company. A _____ will often include the purchasing of the target company's outstanding debt, which is referred to as "assumed debt" by the purchaser.

22. *Answer choices:*

(see index for correct answer)

- a. Quarterly finance report
- b. Registered share
- c. Special purpose company
- d. Buyout

Guidance: level 1

:: Business economics ::

_____ deals with the application of the economic concepts, theories, tools, and methodologies to solve practical problems in a business . In other words we can say that _____ is the combination of economics theory and managerial theory.It helps the manager in decision making and acts as a link between practice and theory". It is sometimes referred to as business economics and is a branch of economics that applies microeconomic analysis to decision methods of businesses or other management units.

23. *Answer choices:*

(see index for correct answer)

- a. Situation analysis
- b. Kaizen costing
- c. Managerial economics
- d. Consumer economy

Guidance: level 1

:: Financial risk ::

_____ refers to the risk of investing or lending in a country, arising from possible changes in the business environment that may adversely affect operating profits or the value of assets in the country. For example, financial factors such as currency controls, devaluation or regulatory changes, or stability factors such as mass riots, civil war and other potential events contribute to companies' operational risks. This term is also sometimes referred to as political risk; however, _____ is a more general term that generally refers only to risks affecting all companies operating within or involved with a particular country.

Exam Probability: **Medium**

24. *Answer choices:*

(see index for correct answer)

- a. Country risk
- b. Foreign exchange risk
- c. Financial risk
- d. Deviation risk measure

Guidance: level 1

:: Bonds (finance) ::

The _____ , interest yield, income yield, flat yield, market yield, mark to market yield or running yield is a financial term used in reference to bonds and other fixed-interest securities such as gilts. It is the ratio of the annual interest payment and the bond's current clean price.

Exam Probability: **Low**

25. *Answer choices:*

(see index for correct answer)

- a. Structured settlement
- b. Bond Rider
- c. Auction rate security
- d. Recovery swap

Guidance: level 1

:: Business theory ::

In business, a _____ is the attribute that allows an organization to outperform its competitors. A _____ may include access to natural resources, such as high-grade ores or a low-cost power source, highly skilled labor, geographic location, high entry barriers, and access to new technology.

Exam Probability: **Medium**

26. *Answer choices:*

(see index for correct answer)

- a. Sense and respond
- b. Micromanagement
- c. Robust decision-making
- d. Macromanagement

Guidance: level 1

:: Probability distributions ::

In probability theory and statistics, a _____ is a mathematical function that provides the probabilities of occurrence of different possible outcomes in an experiment. In more technical terms, the _____ is a description of a random phenomenon in terms of the probabilities of events. For instance, if the random variable X is used to denote the outcome of a coin toss , then the _____ of X would take the value 0.5 for X = heads, and 0.5 for X = tails . Examples of random phenomena can include the results of an experiment or survey.

Exam Probability: **High**

27. *Answer choices:*

(see index for correct answer)

- a. Bivariate von Mises distribution
- b. Probability distribution
- c. Zeta distribution
- d. Noncentral beta distribution

Guidance: level 1

:: Financial risk ::

_____ is any of various types of risk associated with financing, including financial transactions that include company loans in risk of default. Often it is understood to include only downside risk, meaning the potential for financial loss and uncertainty about its extent.

28. *Answer choices:*

(see index for correct answer)

- a. Financial risk management
- b. Concentration risk
- c. Trading room
- d. Fuel price risk management

Guidance: level 1

:: Consumer behaviour ::

_____ is a term frequently used in marketing. It is a measure of how products and services supplied by a company meet or surpass customer expectation. _____ is defined as "the number of customers, or percentage of total customers, whose reported experience with a firm, its products, or its services exceeds specified satisfaction goals."

29. *Answer choices:*

(see index for correct answer)

- a. Convenience
- b. Sustainable consumer behaviour

- c. Itamar Simonson
- d. Customer satisfaction

Guidance: level 1

:: Bankruptcy ::

_____ is the corporate management term for the act of reorganizing the legal, ownership, operational, or other structures of a company for the purpose of making it more profitable, or better organized for its present needs. Other reasons for _____ include a change of ownership or ownership structure, demerger, or a response to a crisis or major change in the business such as bankruptcy, repositioning, or buyout. _____ may also be described as corporate _____ , debt _____ and financial _____ .

Exam Probability: **High**

30. *Answer choices:*
(see index for correct answer)

- a. Consumer bankruptcy in Canada
- b. Bankruptcy and Insolvency Act
- c. Personal bankruptcy
- d. Bankruptcy prediction

Guidance: level 1

:: New Deal agencies ::

The U.S. _____ is an independent agency of the United States federal government. The SEC holds primary responsibility for enforcing the federal securities laws, proposing securities rules, and regulating the securities industry, the nation's stock and options exchanges, and other activities and organizations, including the electronic securities markets in the United States.

Exam Probability: **Medium**

31. *Answer choices:*

(see index for correct answer)

- a. Securities and Exchange Commission
- b. Puerto Rico Reconstruction Administration
- c. United States Housing Authority
- d. National Youth Administration

Guidance: level 1

:: Microeconomics ::

In financial accounting, an _____ is any resource owned by the business. Anything tangible or intangible that can be owned or controlled to produce value and that is held by a company to produce positive economic value is an _____ . Simply stated, _____ s represent value of ownership that can be converted into cash . The balance sheet of a firm records the monetary value of the _____ s owned by that firm. It covers money and other valuables belonging to an individual or to a business.

Exam Probability: **Medium**

32. *Answer choices:*

(see index for correct answer)

- a. Offer curve
- b. Benefit principle
- c. Hit-and-run tactics
- d. RevPAR

Guidance: level 1

:: Goods ::

In economics, a _____ is any good for which demand increases when income increases, i.e. with a positive income elasticity of demand.

Exam Probability: **High**

33. *Answer choices:*

(see index for correct answer)

- a. Normal good
- b. Fast-moving consumer goods
- c. Experience good
- d. excludable

Guidance: level 1

:: Institutional investors ::

A _____ is an investment fund that pools capital from accredited investors or institutional investors and invests in a variety of assets, often with complex portfolio-construction and risk management techniques. It is administered by a professional investment management firm, and often structured as a limited partnership, limited liability company, or similar vehicle.

_____ s are generally distinct from mutual funds and regarded as alternative investments, as their use of leverage is not capped by regulators, and distinct from private equity funds, as the majority of _____ s invest in relatively liquid assets. However, funds which operate similarly to _____ s but are regulated similarly to mutual funds are available and known as liquid alternative investments.

Exam Probability: **Medium**

34. *Answer choices:*

(see index for correct answer)

- a. Gracy Title Company
- b. Davidson Kempner Capital Management
- c. Chartered Financial Analyst
- d. Hedge fund

Guidance: level 1

:: Estimation theory ::

_____ is the process of finding an estimate, or approximation, which is a value that is usable for some purpose even if input data may be incomplete, uncertain, or unstable. The value is nonetheless usable because it is derived from the best information available. Typically, _____ involves "using the value of a statistic derived from a sample to estimate the value of a corresponding population parameter". The sample provides information that can be projected, through various formal or informal processes, to determine a range most likely to describe the missing information. An estimate that turns out to be incorrect will be an overestimate if the estimate exceeded the actual result, and an underestimate if the estimate fell short of the actual result.

Exam Probability: **Low**

35. *Answer choices:*

(see index for correct answer)

- a. Estimating equations
- b. Estimation
- c. identifiable
- d. Wiener deconvolution

:: Venture capital ::

In macroeconomic theory, _____ is the demand for money, considered as liquidity. The concept was first developed by John Maynard Keynes in his book The General Theory of Employment, Interest and Money to explain determination of the interest rate by the supply and demand for money. The demand for money as an asset was theorized to depend on the interest foregone by not holding bonds . Interest rates, he argues, cannot be a reward for saving as such because, if a person hoards his savings in cash, keeping it under his mattress say, he will receive no interest, although he has nevertheless refrained from consuming all his current income. Instead of a reward for saving, interest, in the Keynesian analysis, is a reward for parting with liquidity. According to Keynes, money is the most liquid asset. Liquidity is an attribute to an asset. The more quickly an asset is converted into money the more liquid it is said to be.

Exam Probability: **Medium**

36. *Answer choices:*

(see index for correct answer)

- a. Micro venture capital
- b. Liquidity preference
- c. Social enterprise lending
- d. The Second Bounce of the Ball

:: Accountability ::

_____ comprises all of the processes of governing – whether undertaken by the government of a state, by a market or by a network – over a social system and whether through the laws, norms, power or language of an organized society. It relates to "the processes of interaction and decision-making among the actors involved in a collective problem that lead to the creation, reinforcement, or reproduction of social norms and institutions".In lay terms, it could be described as the political processes that exist in and between formal institutions.

Exam Probability: **Low**

37. *Answer choices:*

(see index for correct answer)

- a. Accountability in Research
- b. Independent media
- c. Civilian control of the military
- d. Face-to-face

Guidance: level 1

:: Financial economics ::

The _____ is the future yield on a bond. It is calculated using the yield curve. For example, the yield on a three-month Treasury bill six months from now is a _____ .

38. *Answer choices:*

(see index for correct answer)

- a. Forward rate
- b. Pull to par
- c. Business valuation
- d. Markup rule

Guidance: level 1

:: Marketing ::

A _____ is the quantity of payment or compensation given by one party to another in return for one unit of goods or services.. A _____ is influenced by both production costs and demand for the product. A _____ may be determined by a monopolist or may be imposed on the firm by market conditions.

39. *Answer choices:*

(see index for correct answer)

- a. Lead scoring
- b. Market overhang

- c. Price
- d. Online research community

Guidance: level 1

:: Industrial organization ::

In economics, specifically general equilibrium theory, a perfect market is defined by several idealizing conditions, collectively called _____ . In theoretical models where conditions of _____ hold, it has been theoretically demonstrated that a market will reach an equilibrium in which the quantity supplied for every product or service, including labor, equals the quantity demanded at the current price. This equilibrium would be a Pareto optimum.

Exam Probability: **Medium**

40. *Answer choices:*
(see index for correct answer)

- a. American system of manufacturing
- b. Limit price
- c. Perfect competition
- d. Switching barriers

Guidance: level 1

:: Insolvency ::

_____ is the state of being unable to pay the money owed, by a person or company, on time; those in a state of _____ are said to be insolvent. There are two forms: cash-flow _____ and balance-sheet _____ .

Exam Probability: **High**

41. *Answer choices:*

(see index for correct answer)

- a. Personal Insolvency Arrangement
- b. Cram down
- c. Suicide bidding
- d. Insolvency

Guidance: level 1

:: Microeconomics ::

An _____ is a contingent motivator. Traditional _____ s are extrinsic motivators which reward actions to yield a desired outcome. The effectiveness of traditional _____ s has changed as the needs of Western society have evolved. While the traditional _____ model is effective when there is a defined procedure and goal for a task, Western society started to require a higher volume of critical thinkers, so the traditional model became less effective. Institutions are now following a trend in implementing strategies that rely on intrinsic motivations rather than the extrinsic motivations that the traditional _____ s foster.

Exam Probability: **Low**

42. *Answer choices:*

(see index for correct answer)

- a. Total cost
- b. Incentive
- c. Opportunity cost
- d. Dorfman-Steiner Theorem

Guidance: level 1

:: Goods ::

A _____ is the state of two people or groups engaging in a lasting competitive relationship. _____ is the "against each other" spirit between two competing sides. The relationship itself may also be called "a _____", and each participant or side a rival to the other. Someone's main rival may be called an archrival. A _____ can be defined as "a perceptual categorizing process in which actors identify which states are sufficiently threatening competitors". In order for the _____ to persist, rather than resulting in perpetual dominance by one side, it must be "a competitive relationship among equals". Political scientist John A. Vasquez has asserted that equality of power is a necessary component for a true _____ to exist, but others have disputed that element.

Exam Probability: **Medium**

43. *Answer choices:*

(see index for correct answer)

- a. Intermediate good
- b. excludable
- c. Independent goods
- d. Rivalry

Guidance: level 1

:: Sales ::

The seller, or the provider of the goods or services, completes a sale in response to an acquisition, appropriation, requisition or a direct interaction with the buyer at the point of sale. There is a passing of title of the item, and the settlement of a price, in which agreement is reached on a price for which transfer of ownership of the item will occur. The seller, not the purchaser typically executes the sale and it may be completed prior to the obligation of payment. In the case of indirect interaction, a person who sells goods or service on behalf of the owner is known as a salesman or saleswoman or salesperson, but this often refers to someone _____ goods in a store/shop, in which case other terms are also common, including salesclerk, shop assistant, and retail clerk.

Exam Probability: **Low**

44. *Answer choices:*

(see index for correct answer)

- a. Proposal
- b. Sales management
- c. Selling
- d. Invitation for bid

Guidance: level 1

:: Microeconomics ::

_____ is a microeconomic pricing strategy where identical or largely similar goods or services are transacted at different prices by the same provider in different markets. _____ is distinguished from product differentiation by the more substantial difference in production cost for the differently priced products involved in the latter strategy. Price differentiation essentially relies on the variation in the customers' willingness to pay and in the elasticity of their demand.

Exam Probability: **Low**

45. *Answer choices:*

(see index for correct answer)

- a. Household production function
- b. Price discrimination
- c. Preference revelation
- d. Income in kind

Guidance: level 1

:: Microeconomics ::

In microeconomics, _____ is the additional revenue that will be generated by increasing product sales by one unit.

Exam Probability: **High**

46. *Answer choices:*

(see index for correct answer)

- a. Temporary equilibrium method
- b. Excess supply
- c. Conjectural variation
- d. Herfindahl index

Guidance: level 1

:: Health economics ::

The _____ was an experimental study of health care costs, utilization and outcomes in the United States, which assigned people randomly to different kinds of plans and followed their behavior, from 1974 to 1982. Because it was a randomized controlled trial, it provided stronger evidence than the more common observational studies. It concluded that cost sharing reduced "inappropriate or unnecessary" medical care , but also reduced "appropriate or needed" medical care.

Exam Probability: **Medium**

47. *Answer choices:*

(see index for correct answer)

- a. Health care reform debate in the United States
- b. National health insurance
- c. Quality-adjusted life year

- d. RAND Health Insurance Experiment

Guidance: level 1

:: Interest rates ::

An _____ is the amount of interest due per period, as a proportion of the amount lent, deposited or borrowed . The total interest on an amount lent or borrowed depends on the principal sum, the _____ , the compounding frequency, and the length of time over which it is lent, deposited or borrowed.

Exam Probability: **High**

48. *Answer choices:*

(see index for correct answer)

- a. Overnight rate
- b. Forward interest rate
- c. Bank rate
- d. Time preference

Guidance: level 1

:: Derivatives (finance) ::

A _____ , also known as a repo, is a form of short-term borrowing, mainly in government securities. The dealer sells the underlying security to investors and buys them back shortly afterwards, usually the following day, at a slightly higher price.

Exam Probability: **Medium**

49. *Answer choices:*

(see index for correct answer)

- a. Repurchase agreement
- b. OneChicago
- c. Area yield options contract
- d. Forward-forward agreement

Guidance: level 1

:: Economics curves ::

In microeconomics, an _____ describes how household expenditure on a particular good or service varies with household income. There are two varieties of _____ s. Budget share _____ s describe how the proportion of household income spent on a good varies with income. Alternatively, _____ s can also describe how real expenditure varies with household income. They are named after the German statistician Ernst Engel , who was the first to investigate this relationship between goods expenditure and income systematically in 1857. The best-known single result from the article is Engel's law which states that the poorer a family is, the larger the budget share it spends on nourishment.

50. *Answer choices:*

(see index for correct answer)

- a. Laffer curve
- b. Beveridge curve
- c. Engel curve
- d. Marginal propensity to save

Guidance: level 1

:: Credit ::

A _____ is a party that has a claim on the services of a second party. It is a person or institution to whom money is owed. The first party, in general, has provided some property or service to the second party under the assumption that the second party will return an equivalent property and service. The second party is frequently called a debtor or borrower. The first party is called the _____ , which is the lender of property, service, or money.

Exam Probability: **Medium**

51. *Answer choices:*

(see index for correct answer)

- a. Senior stretch loan

- b. Creditor
- c. Fair Credit Billing Act
- d. ACA International

Guidance: level 1

:: Marketing ::

_____ is "commercial competition characterized by the repeated cutting of prices below those of competitors". One competitor will lower its price, then others will lower their prices to match. If one of them reduces their price again, a new round of reductions starts. In the short term, _____ s are good for buyers, who can take advantage of lower prices. Often they are not good for the companies involved because the lower prices reduce profit margins and can threaten their survival.

Exam Probability: **Medium**

52. *Answer choices:*

(see index for correct answer)

- a. The customer is always right
- b. Price war
- c. Customer dynamics
- d. Penetration pricing

Guidance: level 1

:: Corporate finance ::

_____ is a form of stock which may have any combination of features not possessed by common stock including properties of both an equity and a debt instrument, and is generally considered a hybrid instrument. _____ s are senior to common stock, but subordinate to bonds in terms of claim and may have priority over common stock in the payment of dividends and upon liquidation. Terms of the _____ are described in the issuing company's articles of association or articles of incorporation.

Exam Probability: **Low**

53. *Answer choices:*

(see index for correct answer)

- a. Corporate promoter
- b. Debtor-in-possession financing
- c. Preferred stock
- d. Fraudulent conveyance

Guidance: level 1

:: Financial markets ::

In finance, the _____ is a model used to determine a theoretically appropriate required rate of return of an asset, to make decisions about adding assets to a well-diversified portfolio.

54. *Answer choices:*

(see index for correct answer)

- a. Clearing balance requirement
- b. Capital asset pricing model
- c. Convenience yield
- d. Crossinvest

Guidance: level 1

:: Dividends ::

A _____ is a payment made by a corporation to its shareholders, usually as a distribution of profits. When a corporation earns a profit or surplus, the corporation is able to re-invest the profit in the business and pay a proportion of the profit as a _____ to shareholders. Distribution to shareholders may be in cash or, if the corporation has a _____ reinvestment plan, the amount can be paid by the issue of further shares or share repurchase. When _____ s are paid, shareholders typically must pay income taxes, and the corporation does not receive a corporate income tax deduction for the _____ payments.

55. *Answer choices:*

(see index for correct answer)

- a. Dividend tax
- b. Dividend
- c. Dividend cover
- d. Towne v. Eisner

Guidance: level 1

:: Economics terminology ::

In economics, an externality is the cost or benefit that affects a party who did not choose to incur that cost or benefit. Externalities often occur when a product or service's price equilibrium cannot reflect the true costs and benefits of that product or service. This causes the externality competitive equilibrium to not be a Pareto optimality.

Exam Probability: **Medium**

56. *Answer choices:*

<small>(see index for correct answer)</small>

- a. Economics imperialism
- b. External cost
- c. transformation curve
- d. Obsolescence

Guidance: level 1

:: Insurance ::

_____ services are provided by some large financial institutions, such as banks, or insurance or investment houses, whereby they guarantee payment in case of damage or financial loss and accept the financial risk for liability arising from such guarantee. An _____ arrangement may be created in a number of situations including insurance, issue of securities in a public offering, and bank lending, among others. The person or institution that agrees to sell a minimum number of securities of the company for commission is called the underwriter.

Exam Probability: **High**

57. *Answer choices:*

(see index for correct answer)

- a. Incurred but not reported
- b. Insurance
- c. Premium Financing
- d. Underwriting

Guidance: level 1

:: Financial economics ::

_____ is a term related to the inter-party relationships of a transaction. It is usually defined as the extent to which the investments made to support a particular transaction have a higher value to that transaction than they would have if they were redeployed for any other purpose. _____ has been extensively studied in a variety of management and economics areas such as marketing, accounting, organizational behavior and management information systems.

Exam Probability: **Medium**

58. *Answer choices:*

(see index for correct answer)

- a. Monopoly price
- b. Asset specificity
- c. Deutsche Bank Prize in Financial Economics
- d. Business contract hire

Guidance: level 1

:: Financial risk ::

The _____ on a financial investment is the expected value of its return . It is a measure of the center of the distribution of the random variable that is the return.

Exam Probability: **Low**

59. *Answer choices:*

(see index for correct answer)

- a. Expected return
- b. Foreign exchange risk
- c. Coherent risk measure
- d. Time at risk

Guidance: level 1

International economics

International economics is concerned with the effects upon economic activity from international differences in productive resources and consumer preferences and the international institutions that affect them. It seeks to explain the patterns and consequences of transactions and interactions between the inhabitants of different countries, including trade, investment and migration.

:: Microeconomics ::

In economics, _____ , resources, or inputs are what is used in the production process to produce output—that is, finished goods and services. The utilized amounts of the various inputs determine the quantity of output according to the relationship called the production function. There are three basic resources or _____ : land, labor, and capital. The factors are also frequently labeled "producer goods or services" to distinguish them from the goods or services purchased by consumers, which are frequently labeled "consumer goods".

Exam Probability: **High**

1. *Answer choices:*

(see index for correct answer)

- a. Monty Hall problem
- b. Production set
- c. Factors of production
- d. Relative price

Guidance: level 1

:: Economic growth ::

_____ is the increase in the inflation-adjusted market value of the goods and services produced by an economy over time. It is conventionally measured as the percent rate of increase in real gross domestic product, or real GDP.

2. *Answer choices:*

(see index for correct answer)

- a. Turnpike theory
- b. Inada conditions
- c. Community capitalism
- d. endogenous growth

Guidance: level 1

:: World Trade Organization ::

The _____ , or GSP, is a preferential tariff system which provides tariff reduction on various products. The concept of gsp is very different from the concept of MFN. MFN status provides equal treatment in the case of tariff being imposed by a nation but in case of gsp differential tariff could be imposed by a nation on various country whether it is a developed country or a developing country. Both the rules comes under the purview of wto.

Exam Probability: **High**

3. *Answer choices:*

(see index for correct answer)

- a. Bombardier Aerospace and Embraer S.A. government subsidy controversy

- b. Generalized System of Preferences
- c. Bali Package
- d. Member states of the World Trade Organization

Guidance: level 1

:: International trade ::

A _____ , or maquila , is a company that allows factories to be largely duty free and tariff-free. These factories take raw materials and assemble, manufacture, or process them and export the finished product. These factories and systems are present throughout Latin America, including Mexico, Nicaragua, and El Salvador. Specific programs and laws have made Mexico's maquila industry grow rapidly.

Exam Probability: **Medium**

4. *Answer choices:*

(see index for correct answer)

- a. Maquiladora
- b. Park In-chon
- c. Authorized economic operator
- d. Vent for surplus

Guidance: level 1

:: International trade ::

_____ is the process of a company increasing production of goods or services at the same part of the supply chain. A company may do this via internal expansion, acquisition or merger.

Exam Probability: **Low**

5. *Answer choices:*

(see index for correct answer)

- a. Horizontal integration
- b. ATR.1 certificate
- c. Reimportation
- d. Outward Processing Arrangement

Guidance: level 1

:: Index numbers ::

_____ is a technique to adjust income payments by means of a price index, in order to maintain the purchasing power of the public after inflation, while de _____ is the unwinding of _____ .

Exam Probability: **High**

6. *Answer choices:*

(see index for correct answer)

- a. Indexation
- b. Isolation index
- c. Corporate Equality Index
- d. GDP deflator

Guidance: level 1

:: Energy crises ::

The _____ began on June 6, 1967, the second day of the Six-Day War, with a joint Arab decision to deter any countries from supporting Israel militarily. Several Middle Eastern countries eventually limited their oil shipments, some embargoing only the United States and the United Kingdom, while others placed a total ban on oil exports. The Oil Embargo did not significantly decrease the amount of oil available in the United States or any affected European countries, due mainly to a lack of solidarity and uniformity in embargoing specific countries. The embargo was effectively ended on September 1 with the issuance of the Khartoum Resolution.

Exam Probability: **Medium**

7. *Answer choices:*

(see index for correct answer)

- a. 1967 Oil Embargo
- b. Energy crisis

- c. Dark and cold years
- d. 2008 Bulgarian energy crisis

Guidance: level 1

:: Microeconomics ::

_____ is a condition of economic equilibrium which takes into consideration only a part of the market, ceteris paribus, to attain equilibrium.

Exam Probability: **High**

8. *Answer choices:*

(see index for correct answer)

- a. Excess supply
- b. Excess demand function
- c. Partial equilibrium
- d. RevPAR

Guidance: level 1

:: Industrial policy ::

_____ industrialization is a trade and economic policy which advocates replacing foreign imports with domestic production. ISI is based on the premise that a country should attempt to reduce its foreign dependency through the local production of industrialized products. The term primarily refers to 20th-century development economics policies, although it has been advocated since the 18th century by economists such as Friedrich List and Alexander Hamilton.

Exam Probability: **High**

9. *Answer choices:*

(see index for correct answer)

- a. Import substitution
- b. New trade theory
- c. Agreement on Trade Related Investment Measures
- d. Good Design Award

Guidance: level 1

:: International economics ::

A _____ , sometimes called a pegged exchange rate, is a type of exchange rate regime in which a currency's value is fixed against either the value of another single currency, a basket of other currencies, or another measure of value, such as gold.

Exam Probability: **Low**

10. *Answer choices:*

(see index for correct answer)

- a. Fixed exchange rate
- b. Transfer problem
- c. Financial sector development
- d. Atlas method

Guidance: level 1

:: Economics terminology ::

The law or principle of _____ holds that under free trade, an agent will produce more of and consume less of a good for which they have a _____ . _____ is the economic reality describing the work gains from trade for individuals, firms, or nations, which arise from differences in their factor endowments or technological progress. In an economic model, agents have a _____ over others in producing a particular good if they can produce that good at a lower relative opportunity cost or autarky price, i.e. at a lower relative marginal cost prior to trade. One shouldn't compare the monetary costs of production or even the resource costs of production. Instead, one must compare the opportunity costs of producing goods across countries.

Exam Probability: **Low**

11. *Answer choices:*

(see index for correct answer)

- a. Comparative advantage

- b. Tradable sector
- c. Overnight trade
- d. Category killer

Guidance: level 1

:: International trade ::

An _____ is a document issued by a national government authorizing the importation of certain goods into its territory. _____ s are considered to be non-tariff barriers to trade when used as a way to discriminate against another country's goods in order to protect a domestic industry from foreign competition.

Exam Probability: **Low**

12. *Answer choices:*
(see index for correct answer)

- a. Commercial invoice
- b. Import license
- c. Confirming house
- d. Nanban trade

Guidance: level 1

:: Supranational unions ::

_____ is a process in which neighboring states enter into an agreement in order to upgrade cooperation through common institutions and rules. The objectives of the agreement could range from economic to political to environmental, although it has typically taken the form of a political economy initiative where commercial interests are the focus for achieving broader socio-political and security objectives, as defined by national governments. _____ has been organized either via supranational institutional structures or through intergovernmental decision-making, or a combination of both.

Exam Probability: **High**

13. *Answer choices:*

(see index for correct answer)

- a. Regional integration
- b. Atlantic Union
- c. Regional integration law
- d. Central American Integration System

Guidance: level 1

:: Economic history ::

The _____ , announced in December 1971, created a new dollar standard, whereby the currencies of a number of industrialized nations were pegged to the US dollar. These currencies were allowed to fluctuate by 2.25% against the dollar. The _____ was created by the Group of Ten nations raised the price of gold to 38 dollars, an 8.5% increase over the previous price at which was the US government had promised to redeem dollars for gold. In effect, the changing gold price devalued the dollar by 7.9%.

Exam Probability: **Low**

14. *Answer choices:*

(see index for correct answer)

- a. Gold points
- b. Smithsonian Agreement
- c. Craft
- d. International monetary conferences

Guidance: level 1

:: E-commerce ::

_____ is the removal of intermediaries in economics from a supply chain, or cutting out the middlemen in connection with a transaction or a series of transactions. Instead of going through traditional distribution channels, which had some type of intermediary , companies may now deal with customers directly, for example via the Internet. Hence, the use of factory direct and direct from the factory to mean the same thing.

15. *Answer choices:*

(see index for correct answer)

- a. Spamming
- b. Disintermediation
- c. Automated Clearing House
- d. EFaktura

Guidance: level 1

:: Accounting terminology ::

In financial accounting, a _____ or statement of financial position or statement of financial condition is a summary of the financial balances of an individual or organization, whether it be a sole proprietorship, a business partnership, a corporation, private limited company or other organization such as Government or not-for-profit entity. Assets, liabilities and ownership equity are listed as of a specific date, such as the end of its financial year. A _____ is often described as a "snapshot of a company`s financial condition". Of the four basic financial statements, the _____ is the only statement which applies to a single point in time of a business` calendar year.

Exam Probability: **High**

16. *Answer choices:*

(see index for correct answer)

- a. Stranded asset
- b. Profit and loss statement
- c. Balance sheet
- d. Revenue recognition

Guidance: level 1

:: International trade ::

A _____ must be introduced when a group of countries forms a customs union. The same customs duties, import quotas, preferences or other non-tariff barriers to trade apply to all goods entering the area, regardless of which country within the area they are entering. It is designed to end re-exportation; but it may also inhibit imports from countries outside the customs union and thereby diminish consumer choice and support protectionism of industries based within the customs union. The _____ is a mild form of economic union but may lead to further types of economic integration. In addition to having the same customs duties, the countries may have other common trade policies, such as having the same quotas, preferences or other non-tariff trade regulations apply to all goods entering the area, regardless of which country, within the area, they are entering.

Exam Probability: **Low**

17. *Answer choices:*

(see index for correct answer)

- a. Intra-industry trade
- b. International free trade agreement

- c. Agreement on the Application of Sanitary and Phytosanitary Measures
- d. Common external tariff

Guidance: level 1

:: International economic organizations ::

The _____ was an intergovernmental organization created to promote cooperation among newly independent states in Francophone Africa. The organization derives its name from the name of the continent of Africa and from the former Malagasy Republic, now Madagascar. The organization went defunct in 1985.

Exam Probability: **Medium**

18. *Answer choices:*

(see index for correct answer)

- a. Asia Pacific Exchange and Co-operation Foundation
- b. Economic Cooperation Organization
- c. African and Malagasy Union
- d. International Clearing Union

Guidance: level 1

:: Foreign exchange market ::

The _____ is the top-level foreign exchange market where banks exchange different currencies. The banks can either deal with one another directly, or through electronic brokering platforms. The Electronic Broking Services and Thomson Reuters Dealing are the two competitors in the electronic brokering platform business and together connect over 1000 banks. The currencies of most developed countries have floating exchange rates. These currencies do not have fixed values but, rather, values that fluctuate relative to other currencies.

Exam Probability: **Medium**

19. *Answer choices:*

(see index for correct answer)

- a. Fixed exchange-rate system
- b. Effective exchange rate
- c. Linked exchange rate
- d. Interbank market

Guidance: level 1

:: Advocacy groups ::

The _____ campaign was founded in June 2010, by Nigerian TV Presenter Philip Obaji. The initiative seeks to promote peaceful co-existence among supporters involved in football followership. It draws support from past and present footballers, football administrators, and celebrities, mostly from Nigeria.

Exam Probability: **High**

20. *Answer choices:*

(see index for correct answer)

- a. North American Man/Boy Love Association
- b. CableHell
- c. 1 GAME: Football without violence
- d. Australian National Flag Association

Guidance: level 1

:: Market structure and pricing ::

_____ is a type of imperfect competition such that many producers sell products that are differentiated from one another and hence are not perfect substitutes. In _____ , a firm takes the prices charged by its rivals as given and ignores the impact of its own prices on the prices of other firms. In the presence of coercive government, _____ will fall into government-granted monopoly. Unlike perfect competition, the firm maintains spare capacity. Models of _____ are often used to model industries. Textbook examples of industries with market structures similar to _____ include restaurants, cereal, clothing, shoes, and service industries in large cities. The "founding father" of the theory of _____ is Edward Hastings Chamberlin, who wrote a pioneering book on the subject, Theory of _____ . Joan Robinson published a book The Economics of Imperfect Competition with a comparable theme of distinguishing perfect from imperfect competition.

Exam Probability: **High**

21. *Answer choices:*
(see index for correct answer)

- a. Monopolistic competition
- b. Pricing strategies
- c. industry concentration
- d. Megacorpstate

Guidance: level 1

:: Foreign exchange market ::

_____ is the quality that allows money or other financial instruments to be converted into other liquid stores of value. _____ is an important factor in international trade, where instruments valued in different currencies must be exchanged.

Exam Probability: **Low**

22. *Answer choices:*

(see index for correct answer)

- a. Renminbi currency value
- b. spot market
- c. Band of fluctuation
- d. Convertibility

Guidance: level 1

:: International trade ::

_____ refers to the exchange of similar products belonging to the same industry. The term is usually applied to international trade, where the same types of goods or services are both imported and exported.

Exam Probability: **High**

23. *Answer choices:*

(see index for correct answer)

- a. Antex
- b. Cross-border cooperation
- c. Intra-industry trade
- d. Export subsidy

Guidance: level 1

:: Special economic zones ::

_____ s , free economic territories or free zones are a class of special economic zone designated by the trade and commerce administrations of various countries. The term is used to designate areas in which companies are taxed very lightly or not at all to encourage economic activity. The taxation rules are determined by each country. The World Trade Organization Agreement on Subsidies and Countervailing Measures has content on the conditions and benefits of free zones.

Exam Probability: **Medium**

24. *Answer choices:*
(see index for correct answer)

- a. Zolic
- b. Zamboanga City Special Economic Zone Authority
- c. Dubai World Central Residential City
- d. Free economic zone

:: International economics ::

The _____ is a hypothesized concentration of certain industries in
large markets. The _____ became part of New Trade Theory. Through trade
theory, the _____ is derived from models with returns to scale and
transportation costs. When it is cheaper for an industry to operate in a
single country because of returns to scale, an industry will base itself in the
country where most of its products are consumed in order to minimize
transportation costs. The _____ implies a link between market size and
exports that is not accounted for in trade models based solely on comparative
advantage.

Exam Probability: **Medium**

25. *Answer choices:*

(see index for correct answer)

- a. Technology gap
- b. Home market effect
- c. Bimetallism
- d. Uppsala model

:: International economics ::

A _____ is a transfer of money by a foreign worker to an individual in their home country. Money sent home by migrants competes with international aid as one of the largest financial inflows to developing countries. Workers` _____ s are a significant part of international capital flows, especially with regard to labour-exporting countries.

Exam Probability: **High**

26. *Answer choices:*

(see index for correct answer)

- a. current account balance
- b. Remittance
- c. Single market
- d. Net international investment position

Guidance: level 1

:: Foreign exchange market ::

The _____ or cash market is a public financial market in which financial instruments or commodities are traded for immediate delivery. It contrasts with a futures market, in which delivery is due at a later date. In a _____ , settlement normally happens in T+2 working days, i.e., delivery of cash and commodity must be done after two working days of the trade date. A _____ can be through an exchange or over-the-counter . _____ s can operate wherever the infrastructure exists to conduct the transaction.

27. *Answer choices:*

(see index for correct answer)

- a. Interest rate parity
- b. Spot market
- c. Exchange-rate regime
- d. Ripple

Guidance: level 1

:: International trade ::

_____ is a government policy to encourage export of goods and discourage sale of goods on the domestic market through direct payments, low-cost loans, tax relief for exporters, or government-financed international advertising. An _____ reduces the price paid by foreign importers, which means domestic consumers pay more than foreign consumers. The World Trade Organization prohibits most subsidies directly linked to the volume of exports, except for LDCs. Incentives are given by the government of a country to exporters to encourage export of goods.

Exam Probability: **Low**

28. *Answer choices:*

(see index for correct answer)

- a. Trade Act of 1974
- b. Uttarapatha
- c. Export subsidy
- d. Schedules of concessions

Guidance: level 1

:: International development ::

The _____ is an international financial institution that offers investment, advisory, and asset-management services to encourage private-sector development in less developed countries. The IFC is a member of the World Bank Group and is headquartered in Washington, D.C.. It was established in 1956, as the private-sector arm of the World Bank Group, to advance economic development by investing in for-profit and commercial projects for poverty reduction and promoting development. The IFC's stated aim is to create opportunities for people to escape poverty and achieve better living standards by mobilizing financial resources for private enterprise, promoting accessible and competitive markets, supporting businesses and other private-sector entities, and creating jobs and delivering necessary services to those who are poverty stricken or otherwise vulnerable.

Exam Probability: **High**

29. *Answer choices:*

(see index for correct answer)

- a. Developmental Leadership Program
- b. Chemonics

- c. Columbia Water Center
- d. International Finance Corporation

Guidance: level 1

:: Financial markets ::

The _____ is the informal over-the-counter financial market by which contracts for future delivery are entered into. Standardized forward contracts are called futures contracts and traded on a futures exchange.

Exam Probability: **High**

30. *Answer choices:*
(see index for correct answer)

- a. Volatility arbitrage
- b. Consolidated Quotation System
- c. Commodity market
- d. Power Plus Pro

Guidance: level 1

:: Comecon ::

The Council for Mutual Economic Assistance was an economic organization from 1949 to 1991 under the leadership of the Soviet Union that comprised the countries of the Eastern Bloc along with a number of communist states elsewhere in the world.

Exam Probability: **High**

31. *Answer choices:*

(see index for correct answer)

- a. Comecon
- b. Interexpress
- c. Molotov Plan

Guidance: level 1

:: Foreign exchange market ::

_____ is an arbitrage trading strategy whereby an investor capitalizes on the interest rate differential between two countries by using a forward contract to cover exchange rate risk. Using forward contracts enables arbitrageurs such as individual investors or banks to make use of the forward premium to earn a riskless profit from discrepancies between two countries' interest rates. The opportunity to earn riskless profits arises from the reality that the interest rate parity condition does not constantly hold. When spot and forward exchange rate markets are not in a state of equilibrium, investors will no longer be indifferent among the available interest rates in two countries and will invest in whichever currency offers a higher rate of return. Economists have discovered various factors which affect the occurrence of deviations from covered interest rate parity and the fleeting nature of _____ opportunities, such as differing characteristics of assets, varying frequencies of time series data, and the transaction costs associated with arbitrage trading strategies.

Exam Probability: **Low**

32. *Answer choices:*

(see index for correct answer)

- a. Dollar hegemony
- b. Snake in the tunnel
- c. Renminbi currency value
- d. Covered interest arbitrage

Guidance: level 1

:: Economic globalization ::

_____ refers to the situation where some countries have more assets than the other countries. In theory, when the current account is in balance, it has a zero value: inflows and outflows of capital will be cancelled by each other. Hence, if the current account is persistently showing deficits for certain period it is said to show an inequilibrium. Since, by definition, all current accounts and net foreign assets of the countries in the world must become zero, then other countries become indebted with the other nations. During recent years, _____ have become a concern in the rest of the world. The United States has run long term deficits, as well as many other advanced economies, while in Asia and emerging economies the opposite has occurred.

Exam Probability: **Low**

33. *Answer choices:*

(see index for correct answer)

- a. Global financial system
- b. global financial
- c. Economic globalization
- d. World currency

Guidance: level 1

:: Unemployment ::

The _____ is the name that was given to a key concept in the study of economic activity. Milton Friedman and Edmund Phelps, tackling this `human` problem in the 1960s, both received the Nobel Prize in economics for their work, and the development of the concept is cited as a main motivation behind the prize. A simplistic summary of the concept is: `The _____ , when an economy is in a steady state of "full employment", is the proportion of the workforce who are unemployed`. Put another way, this concept clarifies that the economic term "full employment" does not mean "zero unemployment". It represents the hypothetical unemployment rate consistent with aggregate production being at the "long-run" level. This level is consistent with aggregate production in the absence of various temporary frictions such as incomplete price adjustment in labor and goods markets. The _____ therefore corresponds to the unemployment rate prevailing under a classical view of determination of activity.

Exam Probability: **Low**

34. *Answer choices:*

(see index for correct answer)

- a. Overqualification
- b. JobBridge
- c. Natural rate of unemployment
- d. Mount Street Club

Guidance: level 1

_____

:: Monetary policy ::

In monetary economics, a _____ is one of various closely related ratios of commercial bank money to central bank money under a fractional-reserve banking system. In one version it measures the maximum amount of commercial bank money that can be created, given a certain amount of central bank money and ignoring leakages into currency held by the non-bank public. That is, in a fractional-reserve banking system, the total amount of loans that commercial banks are allowed to extend when there are no leakages is equal to a multiple of the amount of reserves. This multiple is the reciprocal of the reserve ratio, and it is an economic multiplier. The actual ratio of money to central bank money, also called the _____ , is lower because some funds are held by the non-bank public as currency and most banks hold excess reserves

Exam Probability: **Medium**

35. *Answer choices:*
(see index for correct answer)

- a. Shadow Open Market Committee
- b. Liquidity adjustment facility
- c. Excess reserves
- d. Lombard credit

Guidance: level 1

:: Socioeconomics ::

_____ is the amount of goods and services that can be purchased with a unit of currency. For example, if one had taken one unit of currency to a store in the 1950s, it would have been possible to buy a greater number of items than would be the case today, indicating that the currency had a greater _____ in the 1950s. Currency can be either a commodity money, like gold or silver, or fiat money emitted by government sanctioned agencies.

Exam Probability: **High**

36. *Answer choices:*

(see index for correct answer)

- a. Female economic activity
- b. government intervention
- c. Anticipatory socialization
- d. Purchasing power

Guidance: level 1

:: Currency ::

A _____ , in the most specific sense is money in any form when in use or circulation as a medium of exchange, especially circulating banknotes and coins. A more general definition is that a _____ is a system of money in common use, especially for people in a nation. Under this definition, US dollars , pounds sterling , Australian dollars , European euros , Russian rubles and Indian Rupees are examples of currencies. These various currencies are recognized as stores of value and are traded between nations in foreign exchange markets, which determine the relative values of the different currencies. Currencies in this sense are defined by governments, and each type has limited boundaries of acceptance.

Exam Probability: **High**

37. *Answer choices:*

(see index for correct answer)

- a. Currency
- b. Commodity currency
- c. Monetae cudendae ratio
- d. Hard currency

Guidance: level 1

:: Economic integration ::

_____ is the unification of economic policies between different states, through the partial or full abolition of tariff and non-tariff restrictions on trade.

38. *Answer choices:*

(see index for correct answer)

- a. Free trade area
- b. Eurasian Economic Union
- c. Land bridge
- d. Complete economic integration

Guidance: level 1

:: Public finance ::

A tax is a compulsory financial charge or some other type of levy imposed upon a taxpayer by a governmental organization in order to fund various public expenditures. A failure to pay, along with evasion of or resistance to taxation, is punishable by law. _____ consist of direct or indirect _____ and may be paid in money or as its labour equivalent.

Exam Probability: **High**

39. *Answer choices:*

(see index for correct answer)

- a. Certified California Municipal Treasurer
- b. Taxes

- c. Chartered Institute of Public Finance and Accountancy
- d. Public Resources Advisory Group

Guidance: level 1

:: Humanitarian aid ::

_____ is material and logistic assistance to people who need help. It is usually short-term help until the long-term help by government and other institutions replaces it. Among the people in need are the homeless, refugees, and victims of natural disasters, wars and famines. _____ is material or logistical assistance provided for humanitarian purposes, typically in response to humanitarian relief efforts including natural disasters and man-made disaster. The primary objective of _____ is to save lives, alleviate suffering, and maintain human dignity. It may therefore be distinguished from development aid, which seeks to address the underlying socioeconomic factors which may have led to a crisis or emergency. There is a debate on linking _____ and development efforts, which was reinforced by the World Humanitarian Summit in 2016. However, the approach is viewed critically by practitioners.

Exam Probability: **High**

40. *Answer choices:*

(see index for correct answer)

- a. John Ging
- b. MapAction
- c. Site Two Refugee Camp
- d. Humanitarian aid

:: Price indices ::

Its importance is being undermined by the steady decline in manufactured goods as a share of spending.

Exam Probability: **High**

41. *Answer choices:*

(see index for correct answer)

- a. Price index
- b. Retail Price Index
- c. Monetary Union Index of Consumer Prices
- d. Producer Price Index

:: Markets (customer bases) ::

In economics, _____ forces are those acting on economic factors from outside the market system. They include organizing and correcting factors that provide order to market and other societal institutions and organizations – economic, political, social and cultural – so that they may function efficiently and effectively as well as repair their failures.

Exam Probability: **High**

42. *Answer choices:*

(see index for correct answer)

- a. Parity product
- b. Nonmarket
- c. Vertical market
- d. Market price

Guidance: level 1

:: Visitor attractions in Frankfurt ::

The _____ is the central bank for the euro and administers monetary policy within the Eurozone, which comprises 19 member states of the European Union and is one of the largest monetary areas in the world. Established by the Treaty of Amsterdam, the ECB is one of the world's most important central banks and serves as one of seven institutions of the European Union, being enshrined in the Treaty on European Union . The bank's capital stock is owned by all 28 central banks of each EU member state. The current President of the ECB is Mario Draghi. Headquartered in Frankfurt, Germany, the bank formerly occupied the Eurotower prior to the construction of its new seat.

43. *Answer choices:*

(see index for correct answer)

- a. Goethe Tower
- b. European Central Bank
- c. Palmengarten
- d. Opernplatz

Guidance: level 1

:: International taxation ::

In taxation and accounting, _____ refers to the rules and methods for pricing transactions within and between enterprises under common ownership or control. Because of the potential for cross-border controlled transactions to distort taxable income, tax authorities in many countries can adjust intragroup transfer prices that differ from what would have been charged by unrelated enterprises dealing at arm's length . The OECD and World Bank recommend intragroup pricing rules based on the arm's-length principle, and 19 of the 20 members of the G20 have adopted similar measures through bilateral treaties and domestic legislation, regulations, or administrative practice. Countries with _____ legislation generally follow the OECD _____ Guidelines for Multinational Enterprises and Tax Administrations in most respects, although their rules can differ on some important details.

44. *Answer choices:*

(see index for correct answer)

- a. Tobin tax
- b. Tax exile
- c. European Union withholding tax
- d. Transfer pricing

Guidance: level 1

:: Political economy ::

_____ or neo-liberalism is the 20th-century resurgence of 19th-century ideas associated with laissez-faire economic liberalism and free market capitalism. While it is most often associated with such ideas, the defining features of _____ in both thought and practice has been the subject of substantial scholarly discourse. These ideas include economic liberalization policies such as privatization, austerity, deregulation, free trade and reductions in government spending in order to increase the role of the private sector in the economy and society. These market-based ideas and the policies they inspired constitute a paradigm shift away from the post-war Keynesian consensus which lasted from 1945 to 1980.

Exam Probability: **Low**

45. *Answer choices:*

(see index for correct answer)

- a. New political economy

- b. Geoeconomics
- c. Branch plant economy
- d. Water privatization

Guidance: level 1

:: Fundamental analysis ::

_____ s are narrowly interconnected with the concepts of value, interest rate and liquidity. A _____ that shall happen on a future day tN can be transformed into a _____ of the same value in t0.

Exam Probability: **High**

46. *Answer choices:*

(see index for correct answer)

- a. Beta
- b. Period of financial distress
- c. Equity value
- d. Cash flow

Guidance: level 1

:: International banking institutions ::

The _____ Group or Banque Africaine de Développement is a multilateral development finance institution. The AfDB was founded in 1964 and comprises three entities: The _____ , the African Development Fund and the Nigeria Trust Fund. The AfDB's mission is to fight poverty and improve living conditions on the continent through promoting the investment of public and private capital in projects and programs that are likely to contribute to the economic and social development of the region. The AfDB is a financial provider to African governments and private companies investing in the regional member countries . While it was originally headquartered in Abidjan, Côte d'Ivoire, the bank's headquarters moved to Tunis, Tunisia, in 2003, due to the Ivorian civil war; before returning in September 2014.

Exam Probability: **Medium**

47. *Answer choices:*

(see index for correct answer)

- a. African Development Bank
- b. East West Bancorp
- c. European Investment Bank
- d. Islamic Development Bank

Guidance: level 1

:: United States federal trade legislation ::

The act is American legislation closely associated with its chief sponsor, Democratic Senator Robert Byrd of West Virginia. The act changed the disposition of funds raised from duties on imports that the US government has determined to be subsidized or otherwise unfairly priced. Prior to the act, those funds were incorporated into the US budget. The Act specifies that the funds be distributed to the US companies that file pricing complaints. In short, this meant that non-US firms which sell below cost price in the US can be fined, and the money given to the US companies who made the complaint in the first place.

Exam Probability: **Low**

48. *Answer choices:*

(see index for correct answer)

- a. Clean Diamond Trade Act
- b. Reciprocal Tariff Act
- c. Trade Expansion Act
- d. Byrd Amendment

Guidance: level 1

:: Financial markets ::

In business, economics or investment, market _____ is a market's feature whereby an individual or firm can quickly purchase or sell an asset without causing a drastic change in the asset's price. _____ is about how big the trade-off is between the speed of the sale and the price it can be sold for. In a liquid market, the trade-off is mild: selling quickly will not reduce the price much. In a relatively illiquid market, selling it quickly will require cutting its price by some amount.

Exam Probability: **High**

49. *Answer choices:*

(see index for correct answer)

- a. Margin
- b. Liquidity
- c. Secondary market
- d. Financial instrument

Guidance: level 1

:: Price indices ::

A _____ is a normalized average of price relatives for a given class of goods or services in a given region, during a given interval of time. It is a statistic designed to help to compare how these price relatives, taken as a whole, differ between time periods or geographical locations.

Exam Probability: **Low**

50. *Answer choices:*

(see index for correct answer)

- a. Lipstick index
- b. Average Earnings Index
- c. RPIX
- d. Price index

Guidance: level 1

:: Multinational companies ::

_____ S.A.B. de C.V., known as _____ , is a Mexican multinational building materials company headquartered in San Pedro, near Monterrey, Mexico. It manufactures and distributes cement, ready-mix concrete and aggregates in more than 50 countries. It is the second largest building materials company worldwide, only after LafargeHolcim.

Exam Probability: **Low**

51. *Answer choices:*

(see index for correct answer)

- a. Cemex
- b. Cevital
- c. APC by Schneider Electric
- d. Marcopolo S.A.

:: International finance ::

_____ is the branch of financial economics broadly concerned with monetary and macroeconomic interrelations between two or more countries. _____ examines the dynamics of the global financial system, international monetary systems, balance of payments, exchange rates, foreign direct investment, and how these topics relate to international trade.

Exam Probability: **Low**

52. *Answer choices:*

(see index for correct answer)

- a. International business company
- b. Equity home bias puzzle
- c. Bank payments obligation
- d. Trade credit insurance

:: International taxation ::

A _____ is a tax on imports or exports between sovereign states. It is a form of regulation of foreign trade and a policy that taxes foreign products to encourage or safeguard domestic industry. _____ s are the simplest and oldest instrument of trade policy. Traditionally, states have used them as a source of income. Now, they are among the most widely used instruments of protection, along with import and export quotas.

Exam Probability: **High**

53. *Answer choices:*

(see index for correct answer)

- a. Foreign Account Tax Compliance Act
- b. Euromod
- c. Exchange of information
- d. Tariff

Guidance: level 1

:: Credit ::

A _____ is a party that has a claim on the services of a second party. It is a person or institution to whom money is owed. The first party, in general, has provided some property or service to the second party under the assumption that the second party will return an equivalent property and service. The second party is frequently called a debtor or borrower. The first party is called the _____ , which is the lender of property, service, or money.

54. *Answer choices:*

(see index for correct answer)

- a. Creditor
- b. Credit score
- c. Creative financing
- d. Credit spread

Guidance: level 1

:: Currency unions ::

The _____ is a trade bloc agreement by the Association of Southeast Asian Nations supporting local trade and manufacturing in all ASEAN countries, and facilitating economic integration with regional and international allies. It stands as one of the largest and most important free trade areas in the world, and together with its network of dialogue partners, drove some of the world's largest multilateral forums and blocs, including Asia-Pacific Economic Cooperation, East Asia Summit and Regional Comprehensive Economic Partnership.

Exam Probability: **Medium**

55. *Answer choices:*

(see index for correct answer)

- a. ASEAN Free Trade Area

- b. SUCRE
- c. Germain Pirlot
- d. East African shilling

:: Unemployment ::

_____ is a form of involuntary unemployment caused by a mismatch between the skills that workers in the economy can offer, and the skills demanded of workers by employers . _____ is often brought about by technological changes that make the job skills of many workers obsolete.

Exam Probability: **High**

56. *Answer choices:*

(see index for correct answer)

- a. Employment Promotion and Protection against Unemployment Convention, 1988
- b. Texas Workforce Commission
- c. Employment-population ratio
- d. Structural unemployment

:: International trade ::

_____ was a type of tax device allowed under the United States Internal Revenue Code that allowed companies to receive a reduction in U.S. federal income tax for profits derived from exports.

Exam Probability: **High**

57. *Answer choices:*

(see index for correct answer)

- a. Foreign Sales Corporation
- b. Market access
- c. The Product Space
- d. Business English

Guidance: level 1

:: Financial risk ::

A _____ is the risk of default on a debt that may arise from a borrower failing to make required payments. In the first resort, the risk is that of the lender and includes lost principal and interest, disruption to cash flows, and increased collection costs. The loss may be complete or partial. In an efficient market, higher levels of _____ will be associated with higher borrowing costs. Because of this, measures of borrowing costs such as yield spreads can be used to infer _____ levels based on assessments by market participants.

58. *Answer choices:*

(see index for correct answer)

- a. Basis risk
- b. Credit risk
- c. Valuation risk
- d. RiskMetrics

Guidance: level 1

:: Debt ::

External loan is the total debt a country owes to foreign creditors; its complement is internal debt which is owed to domestic lenders. The debtors can be the government, corporations or citizens of that country. The debt includes money owed to private commercial banks, other governments, or international financial institutions such as the International Monetary Fund and World Bank. Note that the use of gross liability figures greatly distorts the ratio for countries which contain major money centers such as the United Kingdom due to London's role as a financial capital. Contrast with net international investment position.

Exam Probability: **Medium**

59. *Answer choices:*

(see index for correct answer)

- a. Tax benefits of debt
- b. External debt
- c. Medical debt
- d. Household debt

Guidance: level 1

INDEX: Correct Answers

Introduction to economics

1. : Crisis

2. a: Household

3. b: Short run

4. a: Labor force

5. a: Private property

6. b: Export

7. : Supply curve

8. : Money multiplier

9. a: Total cost

10. a: Intermediate good

11. : Exchange rate

12. b: Choice

13. : Inventory

14. d: Marginal utility

15. a: Public good

16. c: Dividend

17. d: Security

18. d: Cash

19. : Marginal product

20. b: Stagflation

21. c: Rational expectations

22. b: Human capital

23. d: Law of demand

24. c: Nash equilibrium

25. c: Great Depression

26. b: Government intervention

27. : Rent control

28. c: Communism

29. d: Monetary policy

30. : Competition

31. d: Game theory

32. c: Total revenue

33. a: Determinant

34. a: Keynesian economics

35. a: Coase theorem

36. : Recession

37. b: Deadweight loss

38. d: Resource

39. c: Nominal interest rate

40. b: Market structure

41. a: Price controls

42. : Physical capital

43. a: Comparative advantage

44. c: Factors of production

45. b: Earnings

46. b: Implicit cost

47. a: Risk

48. b: Soviet Union

49. c: Land

50. : Natural rate of unemployment

51. d: Great Recession

52. d: Lorenz curve

53. : Economic policy

54. a: Economic profit

55. : Trade deficit

56. b: Perfect competition

57. a: World Trade Organization

58. d: Subsidies

59. c: Supply and demand

Fundamental economics

1. a: Medium of exchange

2. b: Capital good

3. : Public good

4. a: Economic rent

5. c: Phillips curve

6. c: Real wage

7. d: Short run

8. c: Arbitrage

9. b: Market system

10. b: Vietnam War

11. c: Goods and services

12. c: Credit union

13. c: Demand

14. c: Foreign direct investment

15. c: Aggregate demand

16. a: Wage

17. c: Incentive

18. c: Preferred stock

19. : Law

20. b: New Deal

21. : Theory

22. b: Export

23. d: Corporation

24. a: Crisis

25. : Asset

26. : Exchange rate

27. b: Instability

28. a: Outsourcing

29. d: Bailout

30. d: Productive efficiency

31. c: Lottery

32. a: Soviet Union

33. a: Price elasticity

34. a: Offshoring

35. b: Gross national product

36. a: World economy

37. c: Keynesian economics

38. d: Inefficiency

39. b: Supply-side economics

40. c: Macroeconomics

41. a: Federal Reserve Bank

42. b: Bank reserves

43. d: Inventory

44. a: Central bank

45. a: Standard of living

46. : Purchasing power

47. a: Balance sheet

48. d: Full employment

49. : Monopolistic competition

50. b: Explicit cost

51. a: Security

52. b: Aggregate expenditure

53. b: Financial crisis

54. c: Economic system

55. a: Variable cost

56. a: Relative price

57. : Stock market

58. b: Public choice

59. c: Monetary policy

Mathematical and quantitative methods

1. d: Sampling error

2. d: Population model

3. c: Null hypothesis

4. a: Multicollinearity

5. a: Quartile

6. c: Consumer price index

7. d: Portmanteau test

8. : Marginal cost

9. c: Linear programming

10. a: Operational

11. a: Semi-log

12. : Kurtosis

13. a: Statistical inference

14. a: Econometrics

15. b: Specification

16. : Posterior probability

17. : Business intelligence

18. : Rationalizability

19. : Two-way analysis of variance

20. b: One-way analysis of variance

21. c: Five-number summary

22. b: Autoregressive model

23. d: Scatter plot

24. b: Continuity correction

25. c: Degrees of freedom

26. a: Histogram

27. b: Minitab

28. a: Time series

29. c: Bar chart

30. a: Producer price index

31. : Multinomial probit

32. a: Triangulation

33. b: Explained variation

34. d: January effect

35. d: Autocorrelation

36. c: Granger causality

37. a: Seasonality

38. b: Envelope theorem

39. a: Question

40. b: Venn diagram

41. d: Internal validity

42. d: Pareto chart

43. : Tolerance interval

44. c: Ordered logit

45. d: Z-test

46. c: Zero-inflated model

47. b: Shadow price

48. d: Hicksian demand

49. d: Cash flow

50. b: Seasonal adjustment

51. : Alternative hypothesis

52. : Giffen good

53. a: Income

54. d: Explained sum of squares

55. : Dependent variable

56. c: Star

57. c: Fixed-point theorem

58. : Forecast bias

59. a: Generalized least squares

Microeconomics

1. a: External cost

2. b: Asset

3. c: Marginal rate of substitution

4. b: Purchasing power

5. b: Capitalism

6. a: Price controls

7. c: Contestable market

8. : Rationing

9. c: Authority

10. a: Excess supply

11. a: Production function

12. a: Utilitarianism

13. a: Financial capital

14. : Isoquant

15. a: Scarcity

16. d: Demand

17. c: Wagner Act

18. c: Economies of scope

19. d: Antitrust law

20. a: Reservation price

21. b: Sole proprietorship

22. a: Tax credit

23. : Entrepreneurship

24. : Physical capital

25. a: Derived demand

26. d: Patent

27. b: Sherman Act

28. a: Unemployment compensation

29. b: Social cost

30. b: Congestion pricing

31. c: Monopoly

32. c: Lorenz curve

33. c: Tax incidence

34. c: Adverse selection

35. b: Sherman Antitrust Act

36. c: Renewable resource

37. b: Gold standard

38. a: Fixed cost

39. : Total revenue

40. b: Cartel

41. c: Nash equilibrium

42. c: Economic rent

43. : Market clearing

44. a: Money

45. a: Deductible

46. c: Expansion path

47. d: Economic surplus

48. b: Variable cost

49. a: Standard of living

50. d: Recession

51. d: Club good

52. d: Socialism

53. : Behavioral economics

54. b: Free trade

55. : Wealth

56. c: Implicit cost

57. d: Marginal utility

58. b: Economics

59. b: Resource allocation

Macroeconomics and monetary economics

1. d: Cost

2. : Future value

3. d: Underground economy

4. a: Open market operation

5. a: Financial asset

6. c: Income distribution

7. b: Recession

8. c: Tariff

9. a: Household

10. d: Economy

11. b: Fiat money

12. d: Balance sheet

13. a: Normative economics

14. c: Federal Open Market Committee

15. d: Standard of living

16. : Wall Street

17. b: Required reserves

18. : Cash

19. a: Factors of production

20. d: Bond market

21. : Great Depression

22. c: Public good

23. b: Income approach

24. d: Incentive

25. d: Physical capital

26. d: Bank reserves

27. : Unemployment

28. c: Unemployment insurance

29. d: Import quota

30. b: Comparative advantage

31. c: Rational expectations

32. : Economics

33. c: Government spending

34. d: Supply shock

35. b: Phillips curve

36. b: Market price

37. a: Automatic stabilizer

38. a: Subprime

39. d: Relative price

40. b: Export

41. b: Absolute advantage

42. a: Money creation

43. a: Dividend

44. b: Market value

45. b: Moral hazard

46. : Time deposit

47. b: Commercial bank

48. a: Fixed exchange rate

49. a: Index fund

50. d: Government bond

51. b: Central bank

52. : Arbitrage

53. : Bureau of Economic Analysis

54. c: Price floor

55. c: Reserve ratio

56. c: Economic recovery

57. c: Euro

58. c: Retained earnings

59. : Soviet

Business economics

1. a: Futures exchange

2. a: Commercial bank

3. b: Credit event

4. : Systematic risk

5. d: International Fisher effect

6. a: Exchange rate

7. : Debit card

8. b: Dividend discount model

9. d: Market clearing

10. d: Public good

11. : Industrial organization

12. d: Agricultural economics

13. : Property

14. d: Indifference curve

15. b: Macroeconomic

16. d: Inventory turnover

17. d: Resource

18. c: Fisher equation

19. a: Capital control

20. b: Decentralization

21. d: Model risk

22. d: Buyout

23. c: Managerial economics

24. a: Country risk

25. : Current yield

26. : Competitive advantage

27. b: Probability distribution

28. : Financial risk

29. d: Customer satisfaction

30. : Restructuring

31. a: Securities and Exchange Commission

32. : Asset

33. a: Normal good

34. d: Hedge fund

35. b: Estimation

36. b: Liquidity preference

37. : Governance

38. a: Forward rate

39. c: Price

40. c: Perfect competition

41. d: Insolvency

42. b: Incentive

43. d: Rivalry

44. c: Selling

45. b: Price discrimination

46. : Marginal revenue

47. d: RAND Health Insurance Experiment

48. : Interest rate

49. a: Repurchase agreement

50. c: Engel curve

51. b: Creditor

52. b: Price war

53. c: Preferred stock

54. b: Capital asset pricing model

55. b: Dividend

56. b: External cost

57. d: Underwriting

58. b: Asset specificity

59. a: Expected return

International economics

1. c: Factors of production

2. : Economic growth

3. b: Generalized System of Preferences

4. a: Maquiladora

5. a: Horizontal integration

6. a: Indexation

7. a: 1967 Oil Embargo

8. c: Partial equilibrium

9. a: Import substitution

10. a: Fixed exchange rate

11. a: Comparative advantage

12. b: Import license

13. a: Regional integration

14. b: Smithsonian Agreement

15. b: Disintermediation

16. c: Balance sheet

17. d: Common external tariff

18. c: African and Malagasy Union

19. d: Interbank market

20. c: 1 GAME: Football without violence

21. a: Monopolistic competition

22. d: Convertibility

23. c: Intra-industry trade

24. d: Free economic zone

25. b: Home market effect

26. b: Remittance

27. b: Spot market

28. c: Export subsidy

29. d: International Finance Corporation

30. : Forward market

31. a: Comecon

32. d: Covered interest arbitrage

33. : Global imbalances

34. c: Natural rate of unemployment

35. : Money multiplier

36. d: Purchasing power

37. a: Currency

38. : Economic integration

39. b: Taxes

40. d: Humanitarian aid

41. d: Producer Price Index

42. b: Nonmarket

43. b: European Central Bank

44. d: Transfer pricing

45. : Neoliberalism

46. d: Cash flow

47. a: African Development Bank

48. d: Byrd Amendment

49. b: Liquidity

50. d: Price index

51. a: Cemex

52. : International finance

53. d: Tariff

54. a: Creditor

55. a: ASEAN Free Trade Area

56. d: Structural unemployment

57. a: Foreign Sales Corporation

58. b: Credit risk

59. b: External debt

CPSIA information can be obtained
at www.ICGtesting.com
Printed in the USA
LVHW041333301019
635717LV00008B/870/P